Russell Library
Middletown, CT 06457

A 2140 471511 2

W9-BNH-593

THE

ENTREPRENEUR

WITHDRAWN

THE

658.11
DEB
JUL 1 8 2006

ENTREPRENEUR

The Idea Person's Guide to Building a Business with Other People's Money

D O N   D E B E L A K

Avon, Massachusetts

RUSSELL LIBRARY
123 BROAD STREET
MIDDLETOWN, CT 06457

Copyright © 2006 Don Debelak

All rights reserved. This book, or parts thereof, may not be reproduced in any form without permission from the publisher; exceptions are made for brief excerpts used in published reviews.

Published by Adams Media, an F+W Publications Company
57 Littlefield Street
Avon, MA 02322
www.adamsmedia.com

ISBN: 1-59337-498-4
Printed in the United States of America.
J I H G F E D C B A

Library of Congress Cataloging-in-Publication Data
Debelak, Don.
The risk-free entrepreneur : the idea person's guide to building a business
with other people's money / Don Debelak.
p. cm.
Includes bibliographical references and index.
ISBN 1-59337-498-4
1. New business enterprises--Management. 2. Entrepreneurship. 3. Partnership. 4. Venture capital. I. Title.

HD62.5.D422 2006
658.1'1--dc22
2005033323

This publication is designed to provide accurate and authoritative information with regard to the subject matter covered. It is sold with the understanding that the publisher is not engaged in rendering legal, accounting, or other professional advice. If legal advice or other expert assistance is required, the services of a competent professional person should be sought.

—From a *Declaration of Principles* jointly adopted by a Committee of the American Bar Association and a Committee of Publishers and Associations

Many of the designations used by manufacturers and sellers to distinguish their product are claimed as trademarks. Where those designations appear in this book and Adams Media was aware of a trademark claim, the designations have been printed with initial capital letters.

This book is available at quantity discounts for bulk purchases. For information, please call 1-800-872-5627.

CONTENTS

Preface

Many people are caught in a dead zone. They don't want to work for someone else's company, but at the same time they lack the resources or know-how to start their own company. This book is dedicated to helping people with an entrepreneurial bent to invent their own jobs—and not just jobs that let them get by, but jobs as chief executives of companies valued at $250,000 to $10 million.

I call this unique shoestring outsourcing approach *OPM* (Other People's Money) *deal making*—or, if you prefer, the *OPM entrepreneurial approach*—because not only are most functions outsourced, but the outsource partners put up all or most of the money. OPM entrepreneurs first caught my eye about five years ago, when I started writing columns about new products and innovations for *Entrepreneur* magazine. I interviewed an inventor who introduced six products through his own outsourced business model. He did very little work, made a minimal investment, but brought in nice profits. However, he was one of just a handful of people capitalizing on the new opportunities presented by outsourcing. Today, about one out of four of the people I interview for my column use some part of the outsourcing approach in their business structure, and a significant percentage of those people use some part of the OPM model.

The expense of starting a business is one reason for the upsurge in this new business model, but a factor that's even more important is that so many other businesses are now organized to support people who have generated a winning business idea. I wrote this book both to demonstrate how people have created an outsourcing model that utilizes other people's money and to help readers create their own million-dollar businesses. The bottom line is that anyone capable of selling a concept can enter this exciting new business arena.

The book is formatted as a how-to resource book for people who want to own a million-dollar business without million-dollar hassles. At the same time, it is full of stories and examples so that it is an enjoyable read for people who want to know just what an OPM entrepreneur is all about. Throughout the book I emphasize uncovering opportunities that allow an entrepreneur to cash in either on a part-time or full-time basis using other people's money. The thrust of the book is that opportunities exist everywhere; the secret to success is to understand the process of discovery, promotion, and closing the deal. My goal is that readers will learn how to go out and start their own businesses in 30 to 120 days.

One of the struggles I had in writing this book is that most of the OPM entrepreneurs don't want their stories revealed because it appears they have too good of a deal compared to their partners. As a result, the stories in the book have been changed so that the actual names of the entrepreneurs and their partners are not revealed. However, the stories are all based on real situations and real people.

I'm interested in hearing entrepreneurs' stories for a possible follow-up book or to feature in magazine articles. E-mail me at *dondebelak@dondebelak.com* if you have a question or would like to send me information about the progress of your own project.

Introduction: The OPM (Other People's Money) Entrepreneur

Money Not Required

Steve Jensen ran Shuttle Concepts for seven years. He networked with convention centers, conference organizers, and large businesses to understand their busing needs. Then he arranged the right type of bus service with a variety of area bus companies. Jensen didn't have any investment in the business outside of a small amount of home office equipment, and he still generated a tidy profit every month until he bought out the bus company that was his primary service provider. The convention managers appreciated getting on-time reliable service with just one phone call, and bus companies looked at Jensen as a source of bonus business that helped cover their overhead. With just a modest amount of work, Jensen produced a steady stream of income, making his business an ideal shoestring start-up.

This book details how a person can run a $250,000 to $10-million business from a small office or home. Ignoring small and micro-small companies with modest profits, we will instead explore a process that an OPM entrepreneur can implement to create a million-dollar or even a multimillion-dollar business without committing any significant resources. This approach takes advantage of the new economic world, where very few companies do all their own manufacturing and marketing. Instead, they outsource at least part of their business. Most businesses typically pay their outsourced vendor both for the up-front costs and for ongoing work. The advantage OPM entrepreneurs have is that they won't pay the outsourced partners up front; instead, they will wait until payment is made by the customer, or they might just collect a commission after payment is collected. OPM entrepreneurs take advantage of marketing services and manufacturing groups to run their own "big" business without a big business overhead. This book does not cover how to run a small business without any money. Instead, you'll learn how anyone can wheel and deal a good idea into a significant business without management skills, money of their own, or manufacturing know-how.

Quick success is the real beauty of being an OPM entrepreneur. People don't have to grind out a business for three to four years to generate profits. They don't have to worry about hiring the right staff or raising enough money, because they can rely on other companies to do that. When competition comes, the OPM entrepreneur can simply look for another opportunity. It is a new level of wheeling and dealing that has the potential to create booming profits. The key to a successful venture is the quality of the concept or idea rather than the experience of management. This book's motto is that anyone who can develop a winning concept can also cash in.

The Risk-Free Entrepreneur contains six main topics to start you on your way to success:

1. The OPM entrepreneur concept: how it works, the variety of businesses that use it, and examples of people who have created their own *Other People's Money* business

2. Locating opportunities for all types of businesses, in any type of community

3. Finding the right marketing, service, manufacturing, and service partner providers

4. Structuring the deal so everyone wins

5. Closing the deal and getting started

6. Learning how established businesses can cash in on the outsource entrepreneur concept

My own current OPM project is a variation of the full-scale OPM entrepreneur approach, and it shows how flexible and valuable the OPM process is. The project is selling silicon carbide diesel particulate filters into the U.S. market. A diesel particulate filter (DPF) is an emissions control filter that is integrated into an after-treatment device that eliminates the black smoke that you see pouring out of diesel vehicles, especially when they are starting out from a stopped position. Here are the steps I took to create this project:

1. *Finding the opportunity.* I had been working with a company that sold liquid natural gas equipment that minimized emissions from heavy-duty vehicles. Clean diesel technologies, which clean up diesel emissions, were starting to sell well in Europe, and that success was creating interest in the United States, both with regulators and with industry users. Users preferred diesel technology because it was cheaper and easier to implement. A major obstacle to introducing clean diesel technology was a lack of diesel particulate filters.

2. *Finding the right partners.* Adoption of clean diesel technology had already begun in Europe by 2001. I went to Europe to locate potential suppliers of DPFs, or possibly a company that could produce the filters for the U.S. market. I was fortunate to find a

small Danish company that had been selling silicon carbide DPFs in Europe, already had some technical reports, and had several customers successfully using their product. The company agreed to have me represent the product in North America and to be my source of supply. I decided to market the product on my own, as I knew the market from my previous experience in selling environmentally friendly equipment for natural gas engines. Also, I knew that there were a limited number of potential customers, all of whom I could contact on my own. The product was sold as a critical component of a diesel emission system, and there were only fifteen to twenty system integrators of diesel emissions equipment in the market.

3. *Structuring a deal and signing an agreement.* My North American rights paid me a percentage that was in line with a company's traditional sales and marketing costs, and my experience in the market allowed me to establish a market presence with modest costs. This meant that both the Danish company and I benefited from the deal.

4. *The results.* I signed the agreement in early 2004. Sales for 2005 were expected to hit $1.8 million, and for 2006 and beyond sales should increase more than 100 percent per year. That's significant volume for the Danish company and substantial income for me. Truly a win-win proposition.

I believe that everyone is exposed every now and then to profitable business opportunities. My goal in this book is to prepare you to recognize opportunities when they arise, and also to teach you how to find the opportunities you won't be exposed to and then go out and start your own business with Other People's Money. After reading this book, you should be prepared to launch your own project within months.

ONE

GENERATE BIG MONEY RIGHT NOW: NO CASH, NO EXPERIENCE— NO PROBLEM

Sony Corporation announced at the end of 2004 that it is setting up a group called the Connect Company to capitalize on the digital media market. This group is set up to be a virtual company, accessing groups in Sony for manufacturing and marketing expertise. It is intended to help Sony be first to the market with innovative products (Apple's iPod is an example of such a product), rather than following technology breakthroughs with knockoff products. The task for Connect Company's personnel is to stay close to the market, project future trends, and then create product ideas so that Sony leads the digital revolution.

Sony's creation of Connect Company acknowledges the importance of idea creation, which is done best by people who track the market and don't have to worry about the everyday hassles of manufacturing and selling a product, or selling and producing a service. Sony is practicing the same principles that this book promotes for entrepreneurs who have great ideas but not enough money. Business has become more and more specialized, and that has created openings for individuals to be just like Sony's Connect Company, cashing in on market developments by finding great opportunities and then finding the right manufacturing or service group and the right marketing organization to bring the concept to the market.

This chapter's goals are to introduce you to the concept of the OPM (Other People's Money) entrepreneur, show how the concept is already working in the market, explain how the concept works, and get you excited about a new way of business that allows almost anyone to develop a million-dollar business, no matter how small the investment capital. All you need is a creative concept that you can sell. We'll discuss:

- Types of deals
- The drivers behind a deal
- The structure of an OPM entrepreneurial deal
- The reasons that now is the right time for the OPM approach
- The preparation required

COMPLEX PRODUCTS WORK, TOO

John Stutsman, from far Western Australia, was a medical innovator working a long way from any venture capital companies. He felt that there must be a better way to prevent blockages in and minimize replacement of indwelling urethral catheters. He thought that a cleansing solution delivered by a bellows delivery system would do the trick. Stutsman's company was able to take care of the front-end development, but it wasn't able to take care of laboratory testing, materials development, manufacturing, regulatory and clinical work, or marketing of the product.

That didn't turn out to be a problem. Stutsman was able to outsource all of the further development, testing, regulatory approval, and manufacturing work, paying much less than the going rate, by offering his future business in return. He lined up a marketing agreement with American Australian Medical for sale of the company's product in North America and Canada. Going from the Australian outback to the American market with a complex medical product just proves that the OPM concept can work for anyone.

TYPES OF DEALS

OPM deals have three components: the company or organization selling the product or service (called the *marketer* in this book); the OPM entrepreneur, who usually manages the initial work developing the concept; and the company providing the service or product (called the *provider* throughout this book). Companies might be partners but they don't have to be, and OPM entrepreneurs might provide some of the marketing, manufacturing, or service themselves. What distinguishes an OPM deal is that the entrepreneur creates the opportunity and receives a significant portion of the profits, while other people provide the money and most of the work to make the project a success. Here's a list of various types of OPM deals; it should give you a better idea of the wide range of projects for which entrepreneurs can put together a deal.

1. *Buy and sell.* As an OPM entrepreneur, you buy a product or service from one vendor and sell the service to a company that does the marketing and sales. You may not take possession of the product or service, but you will have ownership for a brief period of time. You will want to negotiate terms from the provider so that you won't have to pay for the product or service until you are paid by the marketing company.

2. *Commission only.* In some cases, especially when the OPM entrepreneur has few assets, the provider will want to receive payment directly from the marketer. In these cases, you will receive a commission for everything billed by the provider. You want to be sure to have a three- to five-year contract for the actual product and service, plus a share of any future derivative and peripheral products or services the partners develop.

3. *Partnerships.* An actual partnership with both the marketer and provider, or just one of the two, offers the best situation for

the OPM entrepreneur, but this type of agreement is the most difficult to negotiate. This difficulty can lead potential partners to back out of any type of OPM arrangement.

4. *Service or manufacturing affiliate only.* The most frequent deviation from a three-way OPM entrepreneur deal is for the OPM entrepreneur to handle all the selling on his own, which works especially well in narrow markets with few customers, or in situations where the OPM entrepreneur can land one big customer.

5. *Broker.* In a broker situation, the OPM entrepreneur has many providers to choose from rather than just one, and many potential sales outlets. The Shuttle Concepts example in the Introduction (page xi) could have been a broker situation if the OPM entrepreneur had chosen to obtain service from three or four bus companies and have his services sold by several convention centers, rather than just one. The risk of this approach is that marketers or providers may not be willing to have a nonexclusive agreement, and one of them could end up entering the market and competing with the OPM entrepreneur.

6. *Project-based start-up.* OPM entrepreneurs do not always start out with a ready-to-go project; it might need more research, prototypes, further design work, or regulatory approval. In these cases, the entrepreneur might start off with a project that is funded by one or both potential partners in order to determine whether the idea is worth pursuing further.

PRIVATE-LABEL HEAVEN

Fred Culbertson knew from his own experience that screwdrivers often slip out of the screw head, and he decided that what was needed was a screwdriver handle that never had to be moved from the screw head. He thought that if he could just rotate the handle back, as with a socket set, screwdrivers would be easier to use. Culbertson believed that the product would be a perfect item for Sears, whose Craftsman tool line is one of the biggest lines of hardware products in the United States. The problem: Culbertson didn't have the skills or money to make a polished prototype, and Sears doesn't typically buy from small vendors.

Still, Culbertson wasn't about to let such a great idea go by. He started by enlisting the aid of a machinist, who made a workable prototype; he found a company in his hometown that already sold to Sears to present the product; and then, when Sears showed some interest, Sears provided to Culbertson the names of manufacturers already supplying private-label Craftsman tools. The deal was done, and now the screwdriver is sold in all major Sears outlets. The final deal has the provider supply a private-label product for Sears, with Culbertson getting a percentage of every sale, both for his product idea and for his promotional efforts in stores demonstrating his new product.

DRIVERS BEHIND A DEAL

Drivers are the characteristics of a deal that make partners sit up and take notice. They are those characteristics that give the project a strong chance of success. Since there are hundreds of concepts that you can bring to potential partners, to succeed you need to learn which characteristics will become the drivers that cinch a deal. Typical drivers are that you know the customer and the customer's needs; you have the ability to manage the pre-introduction process; and you are delivering a project with a low ratio of risk to reward. You don't need all of these drivers to succeed, but it certainly helps to have as many as possible.

The OPM Entrepreneur Knows the Customer

All companies want to quickly respond to and capitalize on market changes or opportunities. Companies have always worried about keeping on top of trends, but the market today moves twice as fast as it did in the past, and companies no longer have the luxury of waiting to see how trends develop. They must anticipate trends and be ready with the right product and services to stay competitive. Companies do everything in their power to have this inside edge, but the fact is that they often fail. As Sony's Connect Company shows, many companies have realized that they are too busy producing and selling products to be able to keep on top of all the new developments. The OPM entrepreneurs with the best chance of success don't just know the market, but are part of the market. An assistant buyer at Bloomingdale's expressed this sentiment well when she commented about a buying decision for full-size designer clothes from a company called Abby Z: "We like that Abby Z is the Abby Z customer herself."

The OPM Entrepreneur Makes the Deal Happen

A second key driver is that the OPM entrepreneur overcomes obstacles and finds solutions to problems. Companies are for the most part slow, bureaucratic, and somewhat inflexible. When a problem develops they have meetings, prepare reports, and get management approvals, a process that can take months. Because even one or two people can cause a delay, the decision-making process often slows down. OPM entrepreneurs, working on their own, can move much faster to discover solutions and re-energize a project. Markets move quickly and companies need speed, and they recognize that an entrepreneurial deal maker can sometimes put companies in the market before they can get there on their own.

The OPM Concept Offers a Low Risk-to-Reward Ratio

The last driver—and, in the end, what might be the most important one—is the low risk-to-reward ratio of OPM deals. All parties in the deal share this benefit. You cut your risk with a small investment, but still have an opportunity to share in the profits of a multimillion-dollar project. The marketing partner cuts its risk because it doesn't have to invest heavily in production, and the provider cuts its risk by waiting to invest until it is satisfied that the marketing partner will be able to deliver sales. Even with lower risk, the partners still have a chance of being first in the market, and a chance of having a product that is right for the market, if you've done your homework and delivered a winning concept.

THE ANATOMY OF AN OPM ENTREPRENEURIAL DEAL

Most OPM entrepreneur projects evolve in an eight-step progression that is easy to follow and that virtually anyone can execute. There is not a lot of magic in the OPM process; instead, it is a simple case of knowing the steps to follow and learning how to implement them. Our motto here is this: If you're smart enough to be reading this book, then you must have the skills and knowledge needed to go out and close your own OPM deal.

1. *Discover or create a market opportunity* (Chapter 2). Companies typically can discover both the obvious new market opportunities and the market opportunities that exist in the current market. OPM entrepreneurs need to either anticipate market opportunities by six to twelve months or have a unique solution to resolve a problem that has stymied the market. The Palm Pilot

is a good example. Companies poured hundreds of millions into the development of hand-held personal digital assistants (PDAs), but no one could solve the problem of handwriting recognition software. The developers of Palm Pilot overcame that hurdle by deciding that instead of having the PDA recognize everyone's handwriting, users would have to adjust to a lettering style that the Palm Pilot could read.

2. *Package your concept* (Chapter 3). OPM entrepreneurs have to sell both marketing and provider partners, and they need to package their concept with a sizzling presentation to encourage partners to proceed to negotiating an agreement. The key to packaging a concept is to focus on the customer, showing that you have the superior customer knowledge needed to create a winning concept. This requires initial market research, with both customers and people in the distribution channel, that shows strong potential for the concept. Most OPM deals take time, and some require more extensive testing or development work. By packaging a concept early, and getting potential partners interested, you will often be able to entice potential partners into paying for necessary research or project development work.

MARKET REALITY

Companies at any given time do have opportunities of their own to pursue, and some of those opportunities have champions within the companies. Your potential partners will only be interested in your opportunity if it is considerably better than the opportunities they have in front of them. Even with an OPM deal your project still needs to have a strong "wow" factor for its market potential, or nobody is going to get excited enough to make a deal.

3. *Locate a marketing partner* (Chapter 4). Marketing partners typically are the ones that make a deal go, because they have the most crucial job: selling the product and producing revenue. Any project is possible, no matter

what the hurdles are, when you can convincingly show that the product will sell, which is most convincingly done by having a strong marketing partner on board. Finding the marketing partner starts with knowing customers and how they buy, and then finding marketers that need the momentum of an exciting new product.

4. *Find a potential manufacturer or service provider* (Chapter 5). Most of the time the service provider or manufacturer provides most of the money to launch a product, or at least bears most of the operating cash responsibility. To agree to an OPM deal, the manufacturing or service provider needs most of the equipment or service capability in place, needs to be of a size at which the project will have a significant impact on its sales and profitability, and needs to increase production to cut its overall costs.

5. *Validate the opportunity* (Chapter 6). Validation includes proving that the market indeed wants and needs the product, that the product or service can be produced or delivered, and that the project can make money. With luck, the preliminary research you do will be enough to sign a deal, but sometimes further research is required to prove that the product is producible with strong sales and profit potential. You have to be careful not to dismiss a potential partner's desire for more information. The validation process offers potential partners an impression regarding an entrepreneur's professionalism and his or her ability to deal with players in the market. Sometimes potential partners request validation to test the capabilities of the OPM entrepreneur.

6. *Create a strategy to keep your position as an OPM entrepreneur intact* (Chapter 7). To receive a full share of the profits, an OPM entrepreneur needs to create a strategy that provides value to the concept's introduction, which should include controlling the project

and becoming the driving force behind overcoming obstacles and problems. To keep control, you also need a strategy to protect your concept from being stolen, which includes knowing how to sign early confidentiality and letter of intent agreements.

7. *Create a deal that is easy to sign* (Chapters 8 and 9). To force action, your deal needs to be set up for a quick start, with a planned introduction date, and it needs to include a win-win-win scenario for all parties. An OPM entrepreneur has two parties who must sign on for a deal, and if one party procrastinates, the other party may withdraw. The best way to overcome delays is to create an action plan that gets the project in the market in a big hurry. Companies might also delay deciding because they aren't sure that they are benefiting as much as their partners. You need to know how to craft the win-win-win deal or partners won't sign on; or even worse, will sign on and then withdraw.

8. *Forge agreements and sign a deal* (Chapter 10). Finally, you just need to move ahead and sign a deal. The key ingredients of any deal are low costs, high potential for gain, and significant spinoff benefits, including potential new products and services for the marketing partner, and significant utilization of existing resources for the provider partner.

THE REASONS THAT NOW IS THE RIGHT TIME

Companies today are increasingly specializing either in manufacturing and marketing to a specific market, or in creating industry-leading technology for a specific manufacturing or application process. What companies haven't learned to do as well is to use their internal resources to recognize upcoming market opportunities. This failure has created a profitable space for OPM entrepreneurs who can spot emerging opportunities and then locate the partner companies with the ability to make or market the concept. Business has even started to use emerging new terms such as *open-source innovation, free trade of ideas,* and *democratic innovation* to capture the new techniques that companies are using to find profitable business opportunities.

Two other new trends have popped up over the last few years that have opened the door even further for the OPM entrepreneur approach. One is the emphasis on the voice of the customer from Six Sigma (the quality-control system pioneered by General Electric that is being implemented by companies across America). This concept has taught companies that they don't understand their customers well enough, which means they can't always be on the cutting edge of new products. A second trend is that product and business concept life cycles are shorter than ever, which means that the success of companies depends on their ability to dramatically cut down their introduction times for new product concepts. Companies either have to increase their in-house staff to meet the new product and service challenge, or they need to look for other options to discover new products and services opportunities.

OPM Entrepreneur Resources

Democratizing Innovation by Eric von Hippel (MIT Press, 2005) is a recent book that captures how companies are starting to recognize the innovation that exists with customers, third-party providers, associations, and end-user groups, and then incorporate that innovation into their own new product development. The book delves into how, even in the face of declining research and development spending, American-style innovation has never been better. Reading this book will quell any doubts you have that today is the day for OPM entrepreneurs.

PREPARATION REQUIRED

OPM entrepreneurs have to sell two things: themselves and their idea. If you can't sell yourself, it is unlikely that you will be able to sell the idea, because the whole OPM concept relies on a partnership that includes you. This means you need to be prepared to look like an industry expert who can contribute at all times to the success of the venture. While this book is a starting point, you will need to do other outside research and make a real effort to keep up with the industry in order to succeed. One reason many of the sidebars in the book (like the one just below) provide OPM entrepreneur resources is to help you be prepared to succeed.

You need to be not just business savvy, but also savvy about the particular market that your product competes in. No matter what your experience level, you can usually develop sufficient market awareness and expertise by proactively taking advantage of the many resources available to you in almost every industry.

OPM ENTREPRENEUR RESOURCES

Free Agent Nation: The Future of Working for Yourself by Daniel H. Pink (Warner Books, 2002) summarizes the status of the 33 million people (that figure is according to the author) who work independently or frequently change jobs, including people involved in their own microbusinesses. Pink interviewed hundreds of independent workers for the book, which provides insight into what your world will be like as a successful OPM entrepreneur.

Trade Magazines and Trade Shows

Trade magazines are directed at manufacturers, retailers, and distributors in a market. For example, a hardware trade magazine would talk about new developments in the hardware market, including new products, new retail concepts, and general information about the state and health of the market. The magazine will also talk about deals that manufacturers make with retailers, demonstrate how distributors work, and often include "best business practice" articles that discuss selling discounts, promotional programs, and standard buying terms. Trade magazines targeted at service businesses, such as air conditioning and heating dealers, will contain information pertinent to the service industry. Reading monthly trade magazines will give you a huge head start on understanding an industry. You can find trade magazines in Gale's *Directory of Publications and Broadcast Media*, which has an index of trade magazines.

Trade shows are a great place to learn about your industry and market. These shows are often run by associations, and they will frequently have a program of committee meetings or presentations the day before the trade show starts. Those meetings are great places to meet contacts and learn about the industry. Trade magazines have lists of industry trade shows, or you can check *www.tsnn.com*.

Industry Salespeople

Every market and industry has salespeople who are usually knowledgeable and very helpful. The best way to contact salespeople is either to meet them at trade shows or trade associations or to simply request product information. When you read trade magazines you'll notice that the publications have extensive sections about new products, or, in the case of service businesses, new services that companies want to promote or sell. You can simply request information for any product or service that is listed in the new product/service section. You are not necessarily interested in the information about the product or service, but in the name of the company contact, which typically will be included in the letter that will arrive with the literature. You can then call up that contact and ask questions such as how the company's product or service is sold, who are the most important companies in the market, what are the new market trends, and which companies have had the most successful new introductions. You might also ask a contact who is especially helpful if you can contact him or her again in the future.

Trade Associations and Chambers of Commerce

Many industries or markets have trade associations, which are organizations that may include retailers, distributors, marketers, and purchasing agents. Trade associations work for the betterment of companies in the industry. They have volunteer committees of members who do most of the work of the association. You can learn about an industry by joining an association and volunteering to be on committees. Marketing committees can be especially helpful for a new entrepreneur, since they typically have volunteers who are in marketing for their own companies. You can find trade associations in Gale's *Encyclopedia of Associations*, which can be found at most large libraries.

Local chambers of commerce usually have monthly meetings; you should try to attend at least one meeting in your town, as there may be contacts that can help you. Chambers of commerce frequently have members who like to help new businesses, and some chambers have active mentoring programs that can give you a sounding board for your project.

Business Assistance Groups

Small Business Development Centers (SBDC) are funded by the Small Business Administration (SBA); the SBDC nearest you can be found at *www.sba.gov/sbdc*. SBDCs often have courses on running a business, and they provide new-business consultants who can advise you about your industry and educate you about other resources in the area. You might get lucky with your local SBDC and find a consultant with extensive industry experience in your market.

The Service Corps of Retired Executives (SCORE) is another group that offers considerable free assistance from people with wide-ranging experience. You can find the closest SCORE group at *www .score.org*.

Buyers and Store Managers

Many stores—including Walgreens, Wal-Mart, and Target—have local buying programs that allow local entrepreneurs to sell their products in a test at the local store. Local buying programs give OPM entrepreneurs with finished products a chance to talk to the store manager or buyer and get feedback on not only the product but what you need to do to sell to the store. Trying to sell the product yourself to a tough buyer or store manager will help you understand what obstacles you will face and what type of marketing partner you will need.

TWO

PULL THE TRIGGER: RECOGNIZING THE POTENTIAL WINNERS

As an OPM entrepreneur, you can tell you're on the right track when your deal attracts big partners, because they are the ones who produce the sales and production levels that allow you to make a lot of money. Typically, at least one provider will jump on board if there is already a significant distribution or marketing partner, so you must learn to recognize when the marketing partners will say yes to a deal.

Timing is the first key in most business concepts, and the same is true for OPM deals. The four ideal times to strike a deal are when:

- A new market is emerging
- A product category is stale
- Companies need to counter significant moves made by a competitor
- Companies need to expand their market offerings to continue their growth rates

Timing is just the start; the second key is having a concept that provides major benefits to the marketing or distribution partner. The types of significant benefits that could close a deal include a

.cantly better product or service offering, a new price point, a new market opportunity, or access to a new distribution channel.

The last significant key for picking winners is that the OPM approach does require a higher profit percentage than most businesses because profits get split three ways. High profits result from concepts with both high value to the end user and low production costs. You might not be able to determine production costs right away, but you usually can succeed if your concept provides something highly important to the end user.

In this chapter, you'll learn how to look for ideas and concepts all the time, and then how to quickly evaluate and score them to determine whether they are worth any of your effort at all. You may need to look at ten to twelve concepts (or even more) before finding one with the right ingredients, but that's okay, because after reading this chapter you should be able to find two or three opportunities every three to six months. This chapter will:

- Demonstrate that opportunities are everywhere
- Explain why marketers are the key factor
- Show how to find ideas you can work with
- List the characteristics of great concepts
- Explain what partners look for
- Cover the requirements for high margins and low start-up costs
- Offer an OPM checklist and scoring system

SIGNIFICANTLY BETTER

John Mengelhall worked for a company that distributed mining and construction piping. He recognized that pipe connectors used on 6- to 24-inch polypropylene pipes were too difficult and time-consuming to connect and disconnect. He found a better way to make the pipe connector, cutting the time to connect and disconnect pipe by 50 percent, but he didn't have the funding to put the product on the market.

His first step as an OPM entrepreneur was to get an $800 million company to agree to an annual conditional distribution agreement to sell $3 million worth of the fittings, provided the product was produced to the agreed-upon specifications. He obtained the order by meeting with a salesperson and a regional manager of the company, who loved the idea and promoted Mengelhall's concept to their top management. With the marketing agreement in hand, he visited several metal fabricators and was able to find one that would not only produce the connector, but also fund the prototypes and production runs.

Millions of employees just like Mengelhall know a better way to do something related to their work, but they don't have the money or the operating expertise to produce the product or service. Often their employers won't listen to their ideas. In the past Mengelhall would have just dropped the idea, but with an OPM approach, he was able to proceed and succeed with what he was sure was a great idea.

OPPORTUNITIES ARE EVERYWHERE: A LOW-TECH EXAMPLE

For the most part, OPM entrepreneurs make money from user-friendly concepts, offering users products or services that they immediately recognize they want. John Mengelhall's idea, in the example above, was a concept with benefits that its potential users—mining supervisors—grasped immediately. The key for you as an OPM entrepreneur is to understand end users and what they are trying to accomplish, and then discover a product or service that could make their life easier. What gives OPM entrepreneurs so many opportunities is that virtually every facet of life changes very quickly in today's world, creating new customer needs and desires that someone has to meet.

As an example, let's take a look at the residential indoor paint and wallpaper market and how it has changed over the past ten years, with a focus on the opportunities that has created for OPM entrepreneurs. Traditional paint and wallpaper, with different styles or colors becoming more or less popular, dominated the market for years. Over the last decade two big new trends have arisen: faux painting, in which people use sponges or rags and glazing paint to create a wallpaper look; and speckled paint, often used for entertainment rooms, where it creates a nightclub atmosphere at low light levels. Recently the market has seen a resurgence not only of traditional wallpaper, but also of the nubby woven textured-style wallpaper that was hugely popular thirty years ago. Given all of these trends, what opportunities might a creative OPM entrepreneur find in this field?

Product Opportunities

Ideas that an OPM entrepreneur could pursue include faux painting sponges; devices for evenly spacing design patterns on a wall; sponges and tools for edging; paint mixtures for glassy highlights; glazing paint applicators; spray equipment for speckle painting; different mixtures for glowing speckles depending on the desired light level; and paint additives to keep speckles emulsified in the paint. For new-style wallpaper, the OPM entrepreneur could also provide tools to better apply nubby wallpaper; various pastes; or even sprays to highlight the wallpaper or to make it last longer. After discovering the need for a new product, the next steps for the OPM entrepreneur would be to find someone to sell the product (which could be a chain of paint stores, a painting accessories distributor, or a paint or painting equipment manufacturer with branded equipment) and then to find a manufacturer who would make the product itself.

Service Opportunities

As an OPM entrepreneur in the service field, you might be a decorating consultant, coming up with a decorating scheme for either faux painting, speckle painting, or nubby wallpaper and then arranging for a painter to do the work. Or you could have specialized painters work on different types of painting styles, and act as a broker to interior designers who find high-end customers who are looking for a service provider. An OPM entrepreneur might just have a book highlighting all types of great paint or wallpapering jobs, which his or her marketing partners (such as interior decorators) could use as a sales tool, and then furnish painters or wallpaper experts to do the work once the decorator obtained an order. An OPM entrepreneur could use this same approach with home-building contractors who don't have the time to put together decorating packages but who want to offer full decorating service to their clients as a way to add value and make more money.

Event Opportunities

Events also have their share of OPM entrepreneurs. An entrepreneur might arrange for a "faux painting day" show at a paint store, with an agreement to receive 20 to 25 percent of all sales the store made that day, and then bring in interior decorators and painting contractors to explain decorating options and pitch their services to customers. This can be done at a series of stores, or the OPM entrepreneur might go bigger yet, and work a deal with a show promoter, who would promote a home decorator show if the OPM entrepreneur could locate exhibitors and speakers who are part of the changing home decorating market. As an OPM entrepreneur in that situation, you could receive a cut of both attendee and exhibitor fees.

Terence Cabot noticed that neither of his grandparents could effectively use a cell phone, because the signals coming into the phone disrupted their hearing aids. That happens because some of the signals go to the cell phone, while other parts of the signal go onto the user's head. That doesn't bother most people, but it does bother people with hearing aids.

Cabot thought up the idea of a small antenna dish that would collect the entire signal and send it to the cell phone. That didn't turn out to be possible, but in his research he did learn of a small disc antenna, called the StratusClear, that redirects extraneous emissions away from military equipment. The StratusClear technology was available, so after Cabot got support from hearing aid companies that were willing to sell the product with their hearing aids to their customers, he was able to find several electronics companies willing to make the product, putting him in business.

OPPORTUNITIES ARE EVERYWHERE: A HIGH-TECH EXAMPLE

A university professor in the Philippines created a system to measure the catalyst coatings in catalytic converters in order to determine how long they last and when their level is too low for the filter to be effective. Because catalysts are made of precious metal, typically platinum, which is extremely expensive, knowing the right amount of catalyst is important to converter manufacturers. As an OPM entrepreneur myself, I realized that this product would have application in diesel particulate filters, which are used to take black soot out of a diesel vehicle's exhaust. Users would be interested in cutting the catalyst levels, because the average cost of catalyst in the filter for one diesel vehicle is approximately $3,000. The professor just had to modify his product for catalytic converters in order to pursue this market. Let's look at how an OPM entrepreneur might take advantage of this professor's discovery.

Product Opportunities

The concept could be offered to the diesel market as a laboratory test unit. There are at least six U.S. manufacturers that would be capable of manufacturing the equipment; the marketing partner could be a supplier of the catalyst itself, or a supplier of other components in a diesel emission system. Another product opportunity would be collection kits, so that emission after-treatment producers could pull samples from their customers to send to a laboratory for analysis. The product could be sold by catalyst companies, by manufacturers of diesel particulate filter systems, or by several groups of manufacturers' sales agents that sell testing equipment to heavy-duty-vehicle original equipment manufacturer (OEM) suppliers.

Service Opportunities

The OPM entrepreneur could set up a testing service for catalyst levels and catalyst usage per mile or hour of vehicle operation. He or she could furnish kits for samples, and send the kits to any of four or five testing labs throughout the country. The service could be sold through any of the sales outlets listed under Product Opportunities. The OPM entrepreneur would sign agreements with both the sales channel and the testing laboratories to set up this service and then receive a 5 to 10 percent cut (or an even higher cut) of all the sales that the marketing partner sent through the laboratories.

MARKETERS ARE THE KEY FACTOR

All OPM deals rely on a producing partner, who provides most of the financing, and a marketing partner, who is responsible for some investment, but mainly is responsible for selling the product. Though the marketing partner's investment is limited, the marketer is the key to almost all of your OPM deals, because you will have lots of trouble getting a producing partner to invest before a marketing partner is committed to the project.

Virtually every market has a staggering number of new products or services introduced every year, and most of them fail. The companies that succeed, with rare exceptions, are companies that have strong marketing capabilities. You'll find, in fact, that most of the companies that are willing to invest to produce your product or service are doing so because they have failed repeatedly to market their own new products.

OPM Entrepreneur Resource

With a minimum of 35,000 to 50,000 new products introduced every year in the United States alone, it is hard to keep up with all the market activity. A Web site from Marketing Intelligence Service, *www.productscan.com*, provides the best, most up-to-date information that I've found for new products for most markets. Before launching any project it is worthwhile to check to see if anyone else has announced a similar one. You can do a free Web search, or search through trade magazines, but I've found the reports from Marketing Intelligence Service, which start at $75, to be useful.

The marketing partner is the sales arm of the OPM group. It can be a number of different types of entities, including a larger company with an existing product or service line; a manufacturers' representative group; a distributor; a retail store chain; or even an individual with extensive industry experience. What counts is that the marketing organization, which could even be just you, has strong ties to the market that will be able to produce quick sales.

FINDING YOUR OPM CONCEPT

OPM deals exist because of shifts in the market, which result from new applications, other new products and services, or new needs and desires of users. OPM entrepreneurs, companies, or others who move right away when these market shifts occur are the ones who cash in on the market. Microsoft is an example of a company that cashed in on a new market shift, and you can do the same. You can increase your odds of finding a product by being very intentional in your efforts to find new opportunities. You should start by choosing two or three markets to concentrate on.

You can't just be a casual observer of a market, though. You are unlikely to come up with the type of innovative concept needed for success unless you have intensive involvement with the market. The best way to do this is by participating in the market as an end user or by working for a supplier, in addition to learning everything you can about the markets by following the steps on being a professional as outlined in Chapter 1 (see pages 12–15). It is also best to choose a market related to your work, hobbies, or outside interests, or a newly emerging market where there could be many opportunities.

Concepts Related to Work or an Outside Interest

Whatever field you work in, it is probably one where many new developments are occurring right now. These could be changes in applications, changes in the way work is done, new regulations or new competitors, other new products, or big changes in the way customers or vendors do business. With each new development, ask yourself the following questions as a starting point for finding new concepts or ideas:

- Is there a way to make the development more beneficial for the market?
- Are there any new needs or desires among end users?
- Is there anything about the development that annoys people and can be corrected?
- Can the price/value relationship be improved?
- What are the next steps in the market evolution of this development?

Besides the field you work in, markets that are related to hobbies or outside interests are also good sources for possible OPM entrepreneurial ideas. People always know users and markets well when they are passionate end users themselves. You may also be a member of groups related to your hobby; this gives you a chance to hear what other people are saying about new trends and developments. To look for opportunities in your hobby or outside interest, ask questions similar to the ones suggested for concepts related to work.

Emerging Markets

These are often the markets where opportunities abound, but you may have trouble locating

Success Tip

Once you pick a market target, Google Alerts can help you keep current by automatically forwarding to you daily e-mail news stories about your market. To sign up for alerts, go to the Google site and click on News. Then, when the news page comes up, look on the left side of the page for News Alert. Click there and sign up to receive daily alerts for any newspaper or magazine articles that contain your key words. When I first conceived this book I set up news alerts for "entrepreneurial middleman" and "entrepreneur outsourcing." I received two to five alerts per day about articles using those key words. This is one of the most effective (and cheapest) market research tools you are likely to find.

them. You don't have time to wait until new markets or trends are highlighted in *Time* or *Newsweek* magazine or in your local paper. That's way too late—you need to be on the cutting edge. One way to find new developments is to periodically check in on the Web sites *www.gnpd.com* and *www.profuturists.com*. The first site is for the Global New Products Database, which includes new product and concept trends (including services) for 30 major markets and 120 market subcategories. The second, *www.profuturists.com*, is the Web site of the Association of Professional Futurists, a group that provides insight into new trends long before they are noticed by most people in the market. Of course, not all trends they identify come through, but they can help to keep you thinking about what the future might bring.

THE CHARACTERISTICS OF A GREAT OPM OPPORTUNITY

Virtually every company has at least a few (and usually many) employees who at some point come up and submit new product or service ideas to management. Many companies also have people in marketing or business development looking for new marketable concepts. As a result, when you present an idea, your potential partners will have many other concepts to use for comparison to your idea. In most cases, the potential partner just hasn't decided that those products have enough sizzle to justify an investment. Your concept must be strong so that companies will believe it is much better than their own concepts. Your concept needs to have at least three or four of the following characteristics to be considered strong:

1. High "wow" factor

It doesn't always happen, but for some products or services people just say, "Wow, that is a great idea." Wireless Internet at first didn't have that wow factor, but once people tried it out in coffee shops, wireless definitely wowed people. Soon hotels, coffee shops, airports, and all types of businesses rushed to add wireless service for their customers. Products or services have the wow factor when they solve big problems, work much better than current products, or just do unique, interesting things.

2. Ability to help customers meet their goals

OPM opportunities exist when people have problems doing a task, or would just like a better way to do things. Weedwackers were a big improvement over grass clippers, because the traditional grass clippers were hard to use. Intermittent windshield wipers are another example; they work great in a light rain, where the wipers only need to run every ten to fifteen seconds. Software service companies that run operations software on their servers for a variety of customers help their small to midsize customers inexpensively meet their goal of utilizing the more sophisticated software that the market is demanding.

3. Clearly understood benefits

Ideal OPM concepts are immediately understood by customers. That cuts down on the sales and marketing efforts required for the product, plus it also accelerates the market's acceptance of the product. A cell phone that includes e-mail capabilities is an idea that people understood quickly, and the concept took off right away. On the other hand, many people are confused about how services for downloading music work, and those services have taken off more slowly than expected. Another example is Amazon versus eBay. Amazon had an easier-to-understand concept, and it took off much faster than did eBay.

4. A total solution

End users, and therefore marketers, want to buy one product or service that takes care of their entire need. For a big party, do people want to hire just a cook, and do all the buying, planning, and decorating themselves, or do they want to hire a caterer that takes care of everything involved with the event? There is a significant share of any market that wants to buy the entire service, because that way the responsibility for making everything perfect shifts from the end user or buyer to the service or product provider. Not only do some customers prefer the total solution, but they also place more value on it. This allows the product or service provider to make a higher profit percentage on each sale.

5. An appeal for customers with passion

People who have passion know what products are available, spend freely, and typically will pay for high-end products. Potential partners like ideas directed at passionate people because they are easier to sell, and easier to sell profitably. High-income mothers with babies often are passionate customers, as are gourmet cooks and people in general who pursue any hobby. Golf equipment manufacturers are constantly putting out new product ideas because they know that avid golfers will buy the new products, even if their existing products still work.

6. Potentially high margins

Companies value high-margin products or services because they can double the amount of after-tax profit. Companies will average a 5 percent after-tax profit if the margin is 40 percent, but their after-tax profit will average 7.5 to 10 percent if their margin is 50 to 60 percent.

How does this work? Let's look at an example. A margin is the profit per sale divided by the sales price times 100 percent. If a product sells for $10, and it costs $6 to produce, the margin is $10 minus $6, divided by $10, times 100 percent, or 40 percent. To put it into a formula:

$$\frac{\text{Selling Price} - \text{Cost to Produce} \times 100\%}{\text{Selling Price}} \quad \text{or} \quad \frac{\$10 - \$6 \times 100\%}{\$10} = 40\%$$

To determine a margin, you first need a manufacturing or producing cost. In Chapter 3 we'll discuss preparing an initial price estimate, and in Chapter 5 we'll cover how to get a cost estimate from a provider that you can use to determine your margin. Margins of 30 to 40 percent are considered on the low end of acceptable; margins of 40 to 50 percent are considered good; and margins over 50 percent (and especially over 60) are considered excellent.

7. A great price/value relationship

When you get a five-star hotel room in Chicago for $50 per night, you think that is a great value because you feel it is worth $200 per night. In the same way, you have a great price/value relationship when people feel that what you are offering is worth much more than what you are selling it for.

8. Substantially higher quality than the competition

To succeed, a new product has to perform better than the competition, at least 25 to 30 percent better. OPM concepts have to really stand out, and people have to almost do a double take when they see or hear about the product or service. Buyers generally are loyal to the products that they are buying until a substantially better product is available.

9. A strong name or slogan

Customers are influenced by a strong name that immediately conveys what the product

OPM ENTREPRENEUR RESOURCES

Fine-tuning your OPM concept so it's just 5 to 10 percent better can often double your chances of landing a deal. Two books that can help you reach that last 5 percent are *Priceless: Turning Ordinary Products into Extraordinary Experiences*, by Diana LaSalle and Terry A. Britton (Harvard Business School Press, 2003), and *Phrases That Sell: The Ultimate Phrase Finder to Help You Promote Your Products, Services, and Ideas*, by Edward W. Werz and Sally Germain (McGraw-Hill, 1998).

or service is all about. "Junk Drawer Organizer" is a great name. Take a little extra time to work on your concept's name before approaching potential partners. A great name is capable of compensating for a product that doesn't quite meet other criteria, such as that it should be at least 25 percent better than existing products. If you are having trouble coming up with a name, consider hiring a promotional or advertising agency.

WHAT PARTNERS LOOK FOR

Companies are becoming more interested than they have ever been in products and services brought to them from outsiders, either other companies or OPM entrepreneurs. Companies have learned the hard way that it takes a strong idea or concept to succeed, and they see that many of today's strong concepts are developed by small companies and individuals. That doesn't mean that companies are an easy sell for any new idea. Two aspects that help a deal sell are that the concept is a good fit for the company and that the concept offers the partner a quick start in the marketplace.

A Good Fit

Companies typically succeed by doing one thing well. They have learned that trying to do too much often leads to doing nothing well. A good fit for a market means that your concept aims for the same target market, customer, price point, distribution network, and type of support network as the company's existing products.

The target market and the target customer should be narrowly defined. For example, if you are selling crimping tools, simply having a target market of "electricians" is far too broad. The degree of definition you want for your target market and target customer is something like this: "High-end crimping tools for electricians working on buildings and industrial plants." As another example in the services field, "engineering documentation packages" (required to outsource production either domestically or internationally) is too broad of a category. "Documentation packages for plastic toy manufacturers" would be a better definition for both the target market (documentation packages) and the target customer (plastic toy manufacturers).

You should always define the target market in the same way the potential partner does. You can get a company's market definition from its Web page, annual report, or literature. If that doesn't work, call the company and request literature; as you're talking to the salesperson, just ask him or her to describe the company's target market.

Marketers do not like selling products or services in vastly different price ranges than their current products. Service providers and manufacturers also like to stay within their traditional price range, as it matches the fit and finish they usually provide. Manufacturers also believe that quality, packaging, and complexity vary by price point, and they often have trouble producing products or providing services at radically different price points. For marketers, the marketing approach and sales tactics, including the effort to make sales, vary significantly for separate price points, so marketers will view taking on a product or service in a new price range, whether higher or lower, as a significant challenge.

Having the same distribution network is crucial to marketers. The distribution network is the series of organizations that a product or service goes through before it reaches an end user. A marketer might sell to a distributor that sells to retailers; direct to retailers; through manufacturers' representatives who sell to distributors; or through manufacturers' representatives who sell to retailers (manufacturers' representatives are independent sales agents who sell products for a variety of manufacturers). Marketers of services sell direct, through sales agents or selling partners. Changing distribution for a new product or service is a major task, and one that most companies won't undertake.

Another consideration is that your concept should require similar product, service, and sales support to what the marketer provides for its current products or services. Demonstrations, follow-up service, installations, warranty responsibilities, calls that require the attendance of the marketer's top management, and a degree of technical support are just a few of the types of support that marketers may need to offer to land sales.

A Quick Start

Companies evaluating a new idea will consider both how fast the concept can be introduced—which is the quick start—and whether or not the concept can lead to future introductions, which may jump-start a company to a higher sales level. One of the main reasons marketers and providers go for an OPM deal is because it can produce profits and revenue relatively quickly. After all, the partners more than likely are entering the deal because they don't have any promising near-term projects. If the project has an introduction date more than nine to twelve months away, the major drawback of an OPM deal—splitting profits two or three ways—will discourage partners from signing on, as they may have hopes of finding their own new successful idea to introduce during that long introduction cycle.

Companies want a boost in sales, but they are always looking for the next plateau—for example, jumping from $10 million to $20 million in sales. Some OPM projects fill a void in the market and are unlikely to lead to further products or services. Such projects have more limited appeal than do OPM projects that are involved in new trends or markets and that may lead a company to a whole string of new products or services.

PRICE AND SALES VERSUS COSTS

As an OPM entrepreneur, you have two major considerations regarding costs. One is your margin, which reflects how much higher your sales price is than your production costs, and the second is whether or not the start-up cost of each party is justified by the projected sales. Your project will look attractive if your margin is high and your start-up costs are low.

Margins

A three-way profit split means, of course, that the partners have to share the profits. This is not quite as large an obstacle as it seems. It is typical for companies to have before-tax profits of 3 to 7 percent of sales. So if a company has sales of $100, it will generate $3 to $7 of before-tax profit. Your partners will probably be content if their projected before-tax profit is about 5 percent. That means, however, that the project needs margins of at least 55 percent (see pages 29–30 for an explanation of margins), which is considerably higher than a common 30 to 40 percent margin. You need to prove that your project can hit those margins. To do so, you have to provide market research to establish what the value of the product or service is to the customer (see Chapter 3), and you also have to obtain quotes or cost estimates from a manufacturer or service provider (see Chapter 5).

Sales versus Start-Up Costs

Marketers and service providers will probably want a one-year payback on their investment (that is, the production of enough profits in one year to recover the money they invest); manufacturers, on the other hand, will commonly expect a two-year payback. This is another reason your project needs strong margins; without them, your partners won't receive enough profits to meet their payback requirements. In my years of experience, it is not unusual for marketers, service providers, and manufacturers to deviate from nearly all of their requirements, including margins, terms, and size of investment, but rarely if ever do they deviate from their payback rules. A business deal only lasts so long, and all partners will feel that a three- or four-year life is a good run for an OPM deal. They want a quick payback so they can profit on the project in its second to fourth years.

SCORING SYSTEM FOR SUCCESS

With a little practice (and some work), you should be able to locate one or two potential OPM opportunities every year. You need to invest a considerable amount of time to make a deal happen, so you must evaluate each idea closely before starting. If a concept isn't ideal, try to correct its flaws before proceeding. If you can't do that, consider waiting for a better concept. Every concept that you evaluate will help you to more quickly recognize strong opportunities as they develop. Fill out the checklist that follows for each prospective OPM concept you may have. Rate each characteristic 1 to 5, with 5 being the highest rating. An OPM deal should score an average no lower than 2.5 for each of these characteristics before you proceed.

OPM CONCEPT CHECKLIST	RATE FROM 1 (LOW) TO 5 (HIGH)
OPM Concept Name:	
Product or Service	
High margins	
Targets customers' passion	
Offers total solution	
Helps customers meet their goals	
High wow factor	
Customer understands the benefits	
Strong name and marketing slogans	
Substantially better than competition	
OPM Entrepreneur	
Good customer knowledge	
Contacts in the market	
Can play a key introduction role	
Has lined up concept supporters	
Market	
Rapidly changing or emerging	
Strong unmet customer needs	
Large enough to interest partners	
Marketer(s) Identified	
Sells at similar price points	
Targets right customers	
Targets right distribution channel	
Large enough to meet sales goals	
Service or Manufacturing Provider(s) Identified	
Has correct equipment or personnel	
Has sufficient excess capacity	
Meets market's quality requirements	
Can fund start-up costs	

THREE
PREPARE FOR SUCCESS: PACKAGING YOUR CONCEPT

Your success as an OPM entrepreneur depends on your ability to sell not only your concept but also your own abilities and qualifications. After all, you want to be involved in the project for the long term, and you want a hefty share of the profits—at least 25 percent. You need to put together a presentation package that focuses on the opportunity you are selling, but always in a way that promotes your own skills and ability to help introduce the concept.

At the same time, you don't want to prepare documentation that is too extensive. When you approach companies, they may well wonder why you don't just start your own company to launch your concept—especially if you have a big business plan, lots of market research, and extensive financial analysis. If you have that much documentation, they will probably think that you tried to start a business but couldn't come up with the money, and that the OPM deal is your fallback position. You'll be in a poor negotiating position if potential partners assume that you tried and failed to start your own company, and that perception will cast a shadow over your concept's odds for success.

Instead, you want to first show positive market research with intriguing possibilities, and then tell partners that your concept seems so strong that you feel it will do best if you partner up with companies immediately to exploit the opportunity. That approach allows you to enlist partners in the beginning phases of an exciting opportunity, rather than, from their perspective, after you failed to raise money to launch your own company. You may need to go back and do more extensive research (see Chapter 6) before you can finally secure a deal, but you should do that research only after finding several extremely interested potential partners.

In this chapter, you'll learn how to present your idea and yourself as intriguingly as possible to potential partners in order to get them to sign a Letter of Intent and a Mutual Confidentiality Agreement. A sample of each document can be found in Appendix B. You can base drafts of your agreements on the ones in the appendix before consulting with an attorney. (In general, you should to always obtain reliable legal advice before entering into any contract or agreement.)

In Chapter 4 and Chapter 5, we'll cover how to find marketers and provider companies to pursue. For now, the goal is to show how you can convince partners that you have a concept intriguing enough to justify signing documents that will allow you to proceed to discuss a potential OPM partnership. This chapter explains:

- Why focusing on the customer is key
- The type of research that excites partners
- How to identify and connect with market influencers
- How to find a role that creates value
- How to format an initial presentation

CUSTOMERS SELL THE DEAL

Tony Mills was a mechanical engineer in sales for commercial and industrial sprinkler systems when he overheard a dentist comment that he wished he could get a noiseless compressor for his new office in a high-rise tower. Tony first collected a list of the sizes and features of standard dental compressors, and then interviewed ten dentists regarding the type of noiseless compressors that the market needed. He also asked the dentists about the shortcomings of the noiseless compressors that were on the market. His next step was to talk to specialty compressor manufacturers that weren't in the dental market to see if they could produce a product that would work. Those companies gave Tony three concepts that could produce the type of noiseless compressors dentists wanted.

Tony's next step was to approach a national dental dealer with 148 offices throughout the country and attempt to obtain a commitment for the dealer to sell the product if the product passed field tests in at least three dentists' offices. The tests went forward, and both the dealer and the compressor manufacturer were ready to sign. After significant back-and-forth negotiating, Tony ended up getting a cut from the compressor manufacturer on all the noiseless compressors sold by the dental dealer.

FOCUS ON THE CUSTOMER

The key to selling an OPM deal is signing up a marketing partner. What's the key to signing up a marketing partner? It's to show that you know and understand customers—what they need, what they respond to, and what they are willing to pay for. It's better yet if you are an end user and a potential customer, and best of all if you are well connected to people who can influence the market. There are many areas where you can build customer knowledge that will impress potential partners, including knowing how customers use the product, understanding the total solution the customers are looking for, having insight into what motivates customers, and having feedback on how customers have reacted to other new products.

A good start is to know how the customers use the product or service, what they like and don't like, the problems they have with the products that exist, and what customers would like to have changed. A next step in customer knowledge is to understand the total solution the customer is working toward, what other products or services need to be coordinated with the product service, how all elements of the solution need to interface, and what new products or services would provide a better solution.

Features, benefits, and solutions are all important, but many purchases are made for motivational reasons, such as a customer's desired self-image, rather than for reasons directly related to a product's features. Many people bought Ford Expeditions because they were bigger than the popular Ford Explorers, and those customers wanted to look rich and important. You will have some key and valuable insights when you know:

- What motivates customers
- Their typical personalities
- Their psychological motivations
- Their desired image

Don't overlook the psychological and emotional reasons that make people buy. Marketers know that these reasons are often far more important than practical reasons for many purchases. If you are unfamiliar with emotional or psychological motivation, check out my book *Infiltration Marketing: Achieve Astounding Sales Increases on a Very Low Budget by Entering Your Customer's World* (Adams Media, 2000), which has an extensive section on psychological motivation.

Another piece of customer knowledge that potential partners will find interesting is customers' response to recent new products, both favorable and unfavorable, including why they feel that some products have succeeded and why others have failed. Often you can learn more about why users buy products by asking them why they didn't buy certain competitive products or why they think competitive products failed. Those answers can help you understand what customers feel is important and point you in the right direction for new features and benefits.

RESEARCH THAT EXCITES PARTNERS: CUSTOMER RESEARCH

Conducting research for your concept helps you in two ways. First, effective research helps you sell the idea to your partner and convinces potential partners that you have a marketable concept; second, effective research helps you sell yourself, because it shows you have strong capabilities that will help the team introduce and sell your idea. The research that partners are most interested in is customer and distribution channel research.

You need to structure your consumer research in a professional manner so that it is believable and demonstrates that you have at least a degree of marketing savvy. Avoid research that just asks end users or consumers if they like your product; that research won't be accurate, because consumers will often tell you they like an idea even if they wouldn't buy it, and the potential partners won't be impressed with standalone research. Instead you need to use *observational, comparative*, and *price point* research.

Observational Research

One type of observational research consists of just watching end users use the product, noting each step a user takes, and then asking the user why she or he does every step. This is the type of research that many consumer giants such as Procter & Gamble use regularly. If you observe four or five users in action, you will notice that they experience and compensate for different drawbacks to products or services, drawbacks they may not even realize exist. I was once the marketing manager of a dental company that sold dental chairs. We did observational research and observed that dentists had many problems with some older patients who didn't like to lie flat. Dentists were twisting and turning and struggling trying to work on these patients. In response to this, our company created a new chair with an articulating headrest that allowed a patient's back to be at 45-degree angle while the patient's head was still parallel to the floor. The articulating headrest feature, which was designed to meet an observed need, helped the chair become the number-one-selling chair on the market in less than six months.

Another type of observational research, and one that is used extensively for service, is exploring how companies meet a need today, how they plan on meeting a need tomorrow, and how they met the need in the past. For example, if you were considering an inventory management service, your observational research would be to ask target customers how they manage their inventory today, and what they feel are the good and bad points of their current systems. Next ask if they are considering implementing any new systems, and if so, what the systems are and what they feel are the good and bad points of those systems. Finally you could ask what system they had used previously and what prompted them to change.

Both types of observations are based on the premise that people often don't realize what they like and don't like about a product or service, how they compensate for the deficiencies in what they are using now, or even what is important to them about a product or service.

INTERNET NIRVANA

The Internet has become a great place for OPM entrepreneurs because it spawns so many opportunities for OPM deals. An added plus is that there are dozens of Web developer firms in almost every major town that can become a providing partner for you. Take Jeremy Turner of GiftCardsOnline.com. His great concept was selling gift certificates for major stores at 25 and 50 percent off the regular price of the cards. Consumers, of course, would love the idea, but it seemed risky for stores, who didn't want to sell everything at such big discounts. Turner's concept was to offer the discounted cards on a lottery type of system. Consumers would sign up at his site for weekly or monthly drawings of gift cards. A limited number of cards, usually about thirty, were available at 50 percent off the regular price; the others, 25 percent off. The retailers then promoted on their Web sites and in the stores the chance of getting discounted gift cards at Turner's site. The retailers would benefit from publicity, exposure on Turner's site, and the chance to get new customers to try out their stores with a gift card. They also could use Turner's service for mailings to people who signed up for the gift card lottery for their stores. Turner receives 30 percent of the value of the gift certificates sold.

When the first retailers agreed to sell Turner's discounted gift cards, his next step was to find a Web development firm to put together and operate the Web site for half of Turner's take. That way Turner could avoid the $50,000 to $70,000 needed to develop the site. GiftCardsOnline.com was doing $700,000 just a little over a year after introduction, so everyone was a big winner.

What allowed Turner to succeed in signing up stores to offer discounted certificates was his research, which showed that people would shop at a new store if they received a gift certificate and that people buying gift certificates would do a little Internet searching to find certificates that they could buy at 25 to 50 percent off their face value. That research convinced stores to try out the program as a tool to bring new customers into their stores.

Comparative Research

This process simply asks buyers or end users to evaluate your product against three to seven other products and then asks users to rank the products or concepts both by value and by likelihood of buying. It is useful to do comparative research for both direct competitors—products or services that achieve the same purpose as yours—and for other products or services of a similar type that a company or consumer might buy. Before conducting this research, ask people to sign a simple Non-Disclosure Agreement, similar to the one in Appendix B.

As an example, consider an OPM entrepreneur with an inventory management system that can be purchased as either a product or a service. Strictly competitive systems would be other inventory management systems. Effective research would have four or five users evaluate three or four inventory management systems, ranking them by likelihood of buying and also by value. The system they think is worth the most would be ranked in first place, and the system they think is the worst value would be last. This research would be more valuable if you asked users why they chose one system as their most likely to buy and also why they rated another system as their least likely to buy. Those answers give you insight into the buyers' real decision matrix.

The second set of comparison research would compare the inventory management system to other software systems, such as customer management systems, financial control, Web-based customer loyalty programs, quality control inspection systems, and in-process production management systems. Using the same methodology as in comparative research, ask customers to rank

MARKET REALITY

Most first-time OPM entrepreneurs mistakenly concentrate their research on competitive products. Companies and consumers purchase only a small fraction of the products every year. You need to consider not only whether your concept is the best one of its type on the market, but also whether or not end users feel that purchasing your type of product is more important than purchasing another type of product. It doesn't matter, for example, that you have a great inventory management system unless many companies feel that replacing their current system is a high priority.

products by most likely to least likely to buy and also to rank them by value. Comparative research lets the researcher know whether a product is better than its competitors; similar products research lets researchers know whether a type of product is an important purchase. The best situation for our inventory management system would be that it is considered better than competitive products, and that inventory management systems are the number-one purchase priority of most of the survey participants.

Price Point Research

Determining the proper price for your product or service is done by using the two-step comparative research process as explained in the previous section, as well as by research with the distribution channel. Your research should show that consumers and the distribution channel place the value of a concept consistently in between two specific products or services. Those two products are already on the market, and you will know their value. You can take your product's price range to be between 25 and 75 percent of the difference between those two items.

For example, if the inventory management system in the example above was consistently placed in value between a system that costs $15,000 and one that costs $21,000, the difference is $6,000. Twenty-five percent of the difference is $1,500, and 75 percent of the difference is $4,500. You would say that the projected price range for the inventory management system is between $16,500 and $19,500.

RESEARCH THAT WILL EXCITE PARTNERS: DISTRIBUTION CHANNEL RESEARCH

Marketers have learned the hard way that selling end users is much easier than selling the distribution channel, which could include distributors, retailers, buying groups, and manufacturers' sales agents. On a scale of one to ten, most marketers feel that selling consumers or end users will rate a difficulty of three to four, while distribution channel participants will rate a difficulty of six to eight. Your partners will be impressed with both your market savvy and your market knowledge when you produce distribution channel research. Distribution channel personnel typically know the products and markets well and will be able to tell you their opinions right away, so usually you can just do an interview. It is useful for the interview to bring at least brochures of the most recent products or service introductions for products similar to yours, including ones that have failed, and brochures for the top two or three products in the market. Then ask the participants why the products have succeeded or failed, and why the top products in the market have earned their market share. Often the success or failure of products isn't due to the product or service features and benefits, but rather is the result of other market aspects such as price structure, market position of other products, promotional programs, or market loyalty to another supplier. When the market success is due to product features, the distribution channel personnel will explain that to you, but non-product-related reasons for success are also important to your partners. You should ask for a product and feature benefit critique of your product as well, both against the market leader and against the category's last successful introduction. Finally, ask people how they think the product should be packaged and what they believe is the proper product price point.

You can find contacts in the distribution channel by requesting literature and by attending trade-show seminars and association meetings. You don't need to do lots of research with the distribution channel—in fact, as mentioned earlier, too much research might convince potential partners that you really wanted to start your own company, and the OPM approach is merely a fallback position. Research with just three or four people in the distribution channel will help solidify your image as being involved in, and knowledgeable about, the market.

IDENTIFYING AND CONNECTING WITH MARKET INFLUENCERS

The two points that will impress potential partners the most are, first, great customer research and, second, connections to market influencers. Many markets have influential people in them that the market looks to for advice about new products or services. Television cooking chefs, or big-name chefs like Wolfgang Puck, are market influencers. Another influencer might be a key buyer for a progressive chain like Williams-Sonoma. Industrial markets almost always have key influencers who prepare seminars and write articles for trade magazines. Not all products or services have people who are widely listened to in the business, but many do.

Identifying Influencers

You will be most successful if you can identify and contact the top three or four influencers in your market, but that is not always possible. Often those influencers are hard to access for a variety of reasons. If that happens, don't be afraid to go with people who have less influence. Knowing any of a market's influencers is still very helpful when dealing with partners. The best three ways of finding market influencers are through trade magazines, trade shows, or trade associations.

Trade magazines often have experts who write columns, or occasional articles, and they often quote the influencers in the articles about the state of the market. The magazines' Web sites will almost always have articles from past issues. Look up the articles and then note the writers who frequently write major articles. You can also call up the writers or editors of trade magazines and ask them the names of key influencers. Trade magazine editors are much more accessible than are consumer magazine editors, and you can usually reach them after no more than two to four phone calls.

Another way to locate influencers is by tracking speakers at trade shows, who often have seminars or technical papers presented the day or two before the actual show starts. Attending these events is a great way to meet many people in the industry (these seminars are also the best way to meet potential marketing partners). Industry or market influencers often give seminars, and the influencers almost always attend the show. At the seminars you will also have an opportunity to meet many people who are experienced in the market or industry. You can ask people you meet there for the names of people who are influential in the market. In my experience, most of the seminar attendees will be willing to share information with you.

A last way to meet market influencers is to be active in trade associations. Such associations often have local meetings

OPM Entrepreneur Resources

When you meet contacts at trade shows or association meetings you have just a few seconds to deliver a statement with impact to get them interested in your project. Three books that can help you fine-tune a great fifteen-second message are *Words That Sell*, by Richard Bayan (McGraw-Hill, 1987), *Phrases That Sell*, by Edward W. Werz and Sally Germain (McGraw-Hill, 1998), and *More Words That Sell*, by Richard Bayan (McGraw-Hill, 2003).

and committees, and, as mentioned in Chapter 1, volunteering to participate in the relevant association's committees is a great way to meet the key influencers in a market, or at least learn who they are.

Connecting with Influencers

Before you can try to connect with the influencer, which means getting to know that person in a meaningful way rather than just having met at a trade show, you first have to interest him or her in your project. At all costs, avoid boasting about what a great idea you have. That will turn off any influencer. Instead, emphasize that you have conducted research with X number of customers and have found that the market is looking for a product that does a better job of _____, or a service that can better handle _____.

Your goal with an influencer is to get to know the person somewhat and to be able to contact him or her when you need assistance. Here are three good ways you can connect with influencers:

- Volunteering to help them at their events
- Hiring them for a short-term evaluation of your product
- Working with them to develop a proposal for potential marketing partners

Influencers present seminars, give speeches, and write articles. They will often allow you to volunteer to assist in any way that makes sense at seminars or events, which helps you get to know the influencer better and also helps you learn about the market and industry needs.

You can also pay the influencer for a two-hour interview, during which you could discuss your concepts and your consumer and distributor research and then ask the influencer for an opinion about the idea's marketability and advice about what steps you should take next.

A third option is to prepare a proposal for a product or service evaluation that would be conducted by the market influencer for presentation to a potential marketing partner. You would offer the proposal to an interested marketer who wasn't quite sure if it made sense to move ahead. If asked, tell the influencer that he or she would receive any fees generated by the proposal. This option is one that might interest the influencer the most, because it gives that person the opportunity to pick up business with a large potential client, and it helps you because the marketer should be impressed that you know an influencer well enough to prepare a joint research proposal.

FINDING A ROLE THAT CREATES VALUE

Because an OPM entrepreneur has continued involvement with a project and receives considerable revenue, potential partners will evaluate both the OPM entrepreneur's concept and the value of the OPM entrepreneur to the project. As you package your concept for a presentation, you need to define your role and how it will help the project's introduction. Selecting a specific and more detailed role that gives you value is discussed more thoroughly in Chapter 7. For your presentation you want to concentrate on broad roles with just a few details, which typically fall into one of three areas: sales help; product development; and infiltration marketer. Other roles also exist, such as engineering assistance or quality control or production management assistance, but they usually aren't as important to potential partners. Before approaching partners, decide on a role that fits your skills, that you are willing to do, and that adds value to the project.

1. Sales help

You could have special contacts in the market with key customers, or you might be able to offer technical training, seminars, salesperson training, or manufacturers' sales agent training. The best sales support is for you to know at least a few actual customers, distributors, or retailers.

2. Product development

Your concept might be taking advantage of a new trend, and there could be further business development work needed to identify future products and service. You are in a strong position to do this if you have made numerous customer contacts, are well connected with key market influencers, or are an end user yourself.

3. Infiltration marketer

You can play a key role by being active in the customer's world for the marketing company. Some of the tactics you can use are sponsoring events, holding seminars, actively discussing the products and services on blogs and other Internet sites, running an advisory council, and attending all trade shows, association meetings, and other events to keep the marketer's name in front of customers. This tactic also puts you on the leading edge for developing new concepts and ideas that you can sell with your OPM partners.

SUCCESS TIP

Entering the customers' world appears to be a fairly simple task that a company should be able to do. But customers are skeptical of companies' motives, and it is hard to convince customers that a company is just looking out for their interests. You, as the entrepreneur, have a better chance of being looked at as having customers' interests at heart. After all, you created a concept that customers needed and then convinced two partners to put it on the market. Being a part of the customers' world is a role that marketers value, and in most cases it is one that an OPM entrepreneur can fill more effectively than can a company. For those reasons, this is a role OPM entrepreneurs should offer to play on all their deals.

FORMATTING AN INITIAL PRESENTATION

Before disclosing your whole concept to a potential partner, you should strongly consider having the potential partner sign a Mutual Confidentiality Agreement, or you could run the risk of your idea being stolen. Remember the example of the noiseless dental compressors at the beginning of this chapter? That situation was one in which the dental dealer management could possibly search out noiseless compressor manufacturers on their own once the dealers knew that manufacturers of noiseless compressors exist in the market. An OPM entrepreneur has the advantage of already knowing who the manufacturers are, and could get the product to the market sooner, but there is still a risk that the dental dealer will go off on his own.

Companies will be reluctant to sign a Statement of Confidentiality if they know little about your project. The initial presentation discussed in this chapter is just to get the partners to sign a confidential statement. You have to give away some information about your product, but hopefully you can offer just enough information to intrigue the partner without disclosing everything. Once you get the Confidentiality Agreement signed you can disclose your full concept.

Your initial presentation needs to convey that you've uncovered an intriguing market opportunity, that the opportunity is immediate and large, and that you've decided that the best way for you to take advantage of the opportunity is to partner up with companies already in the market rather than to start your own company. The presentation doesn't have to be very long; a fifteen-slide PowerPoint presentation will almost always be sufficient. Here are the slides your presentation should have:

1. *Define the target market.* Example: Gardeners and home-owners who suffer from overgrowth of wild gardenias and other plants with running root systems.

2. *Explain your connection to the target customer group.* Example: You spend forty to eighty hours per year pulling out wild gardenias.

3. *List the approximate market size, mentioning a reliable source for your information if at all possible.* Example: According to *Home and Garden* magazine, this problem afflicts more than 20 million people.

4. *Describe how you researched the validity of your premise.* Example: Fast-growing plants with spreading roots are a major annoyance to gardeners. You might mention that you attended garden shows, talked to experts at garden shops, and talked to fifteen people in your neighborhood who all had problems.

5. *Explain in vague terms a concept you created to solve this problem.* Example: You believed that a below-ground barrier with a slow-release chemical would solve the problem.

6. *List the steps you've taken to prove that your concept will work.* Example: You tested your concept in your yard and in the yards of four family members.

7. *Describe customer research you've done on the concept.* Example: Eleven of fifteen neighbors preferred your concept after comparing it to three other options: chemicals that kill all herbaceous plants; easy weed pullers; and other ground barriers.

8. *State the price range that you project for your product or service based on customer and distributor research.* Example: The cost would be $40 for an average-size garden.

9. *Explain any research you've done with retailers, distributors, or others in the distribution channel, listing the number of people you've talked to and listing three or four positive points from your surveys.*

10. *List any market influencers you've talked to, and list one positive quote about your concept from each one.*

11. *State the three options you've considered: working with a marketing and provider partner; selling or licensing the idea or concept; starting a company to promote the concept.*

12. *Show that you've selected option one—working with a marketing and provider partner.* Give these reasons for your choice: first, it is the quickest route to market, and second, it is the best route to establish a leading market position.

13. *State that you've already found two or three ideal marketing partners (if you are presenting to a potential service or manufacturing partner) or that you have found two or three ideal service or manufacturing partners (if you are presenting to potential marketing partners).*

14. *Explain the reasons you have selected this company as a potential partner.* This slide should be customized for whomever you are presenting to. Some of the reasons you might include: the company is well known in the market; it has a strong sales force; it already sells complementary products; it has a highly regarded service network; it possesses a reputation for high quality; and it has the correct manufacturing process already in place.

15. *Give an estimate for the volume of products you think you could be selling in three years.*

After you finish the presentation, explain that you would like to sign a Mutual Confidentiality Agreement and then, when the company is ready, a Letter of Intent. Explain that you intend to negotiate a final agreement with both the marketing partner and the service provider or manufacturer. Bring a Mutual Confidentiality Agreement and Letter of Intent (see Appendix B) in case a company is interested in learning more.

FOUR
SELLING BIG: FINDING THE RIGHT MARKETING PARTNERS

O PM entrepreneurs need to locate a marketer with high-volume sales, but they also need to understand what type of marketing partner will move forward and make the deal. There are several principles to follow when selecting a partner. Potential partners need to be selling to the right market, and they need to be able to generate significant revenue per year with your concept. The partner should also have a strong reputation and have had strong sales growth. But the critical point is to work with companies in which OPM entrepreneurs can find someone inside the organization who is willing to push for an idea and to help prepare presentations that match the company's goals. Ideally this person is a regional manager or marketing person with enough clout to move the project forward. A person inside also helps to increase the partner's support for the project once a deal is signed.

The marketing partner can be chosen from a wide range of businesses: a manufacturing company that makes other products it sells itself; a distributor that sells to the same target market; a manufacturer's representative firm that plays an important role in a particular market; a large end user of an industrial product; or even a major retailer looking to sign a private-label agreement for its stores. The term "marketer" is a loose concept in the OPM approach, because all that matters is that the marketing partner's commitment to take on the product is strong enough to encourage a manufacturer or service provider to fund production. The result is that the OPM approach can be used to pursue any viable concept, especially if the OPM entrepreneur understands exactly what will appeal to the final customer, who is served by all partners including the marketer, service provider or manufacturer, and OPM entrepreneur.

The goal of this chapter is to prepare you to find and approach potential marketing partners. This process is intimidating for many new entrepreneurs because marketers are the key party to executing a deal, and also because they are usually the most knowledgeable people in the market. Here you'll learn what to expect, how to look professional, and how to identify the key points you need to get across to get your foot in the door.

This chapter will:

- Describe potential marketing partners
- Demonstrate how to research a market to find potential partners
- Discuss when partners will be receptive to a deal
- Explain how to choose the best marketer
- List types of deals that might entice a marketer
- Explain who the best inside contacts are, how to get them on your side, and why the contact working with you also will be a big winner

EASY TO SELL, BUT STILL A MARKET FORCE

Jesse Franklin was bursting with ideas for great little housewares gadgets, from a banana hook that hung from a cabinet to a strain-and-serve kitchen utensil that strained pasta while eliminating the age-old problem of pasta overflowing the strainer. He had visions of a whole line of products, all with a distinctive packaging and name to establish his brand. Unfortunately, he didn't have money for production or a way to effectively market the product to supermarkets or mass merchandisers.

Franklin researched the market and decided that his ideal solution was to form an alliance with a supermarket rack jobber in his area. Franklin learned that rack jobbers—companies that purchase space in supermarkets and then stock that space with kitchen gadgets, such as spatulas, ice-cream scoops, and cake cutters—typically average only 35 percent profit margins. The rack jobber might be a good candidate as the marketing partner, since by splitting profits in an OPM-type deal, the jobber would raise its profit percentage by 10 percent. The jobber he approached thought this was a good deal too, and agreed to be a marketing partner. Franklin used the jobber's commitment to encourage three different manufacturing partners to invest in producing one of Franklin's product concepts. Before long, Franklin was in control of a multimillion-dollar business.

Why didn't Franklin just sell to the rack jobber at standard discounts? That strategy would net Franklin a higher share of the profits. The problem with that approach was that the rack jobber could then stop ordering at any time and Franklin wouldn't have had the firm long-term commitment he needed to inspire the manufacturers to make an investment. Increased margins gave the jobber a strong incentive to contractually commit to stock the product for three years.

All right then, why didn't Franklin try to get a larger manufacturer or distributor partner? Because those sales may have taken much longer, and the outcome was uncertain because Franklin's product line would have been a small percentage of the larger partner's sales. Also, Franklin didn't necessarily need a larger partner. The rack jobber sold regionally to supermarkets, and they bought so much product that even a regional rack jobber could produce significant sales. Franklin chose the rack jobber because he had a compelling sales proposition (more profit for the rack jobber) and the sale was much easier than it would be to a distributor or other marketing partner. There was also less risk. Franklin didn't have any patents and couldn't easily stop someone from stealing his ideas. The rack jobber didn't have the resources to produce its own products and didn't have any motivation to just take Franklin's ideas and run with them.

POTENTIAL MARKETING PARTNERS

When people think of a marketing partner, they typically think of bigger companies that have large marketing and sales staffs. Those companies can be good partners, but they are partners that can take a long time to sell. They also pose the most risk for stealing the concept because they have the capability of introducing a concept on their own. What you need from a marketing partner is a commitment to take the product for a period of time that is long enough to get a provider to put up cash to support the product. This is why "marketing partner" is a very broad term for OPM entrepreneurs. For example, a retailer is a partner if it agrees to buy a fixed number of units for three years in return for an additional 10 percent discount and an exclusive sales agreement. By expanding your concept of a marketing partner you'll see that there are many more potential partners than you may have originally thought. You are not restricted just to traditional companies that produce and sell products, but instead can approach anyone selling or servicing the target customer.

Companies with Branded Offerings

Products and services are branded when they are sold under a name that the company promotes. The Geek Squad sells branded computer repair services, and the Crank Brothers sell branded bike repair products to bike shops. Companies with branded products typically sell through established distribution channels, compete with many other companies, and have a somewhat steady stream of business. These companies will be interested in OPM deals when those deals improve their competitive situation.

Distributors

A market fact that makes distributors good OPM prospects is that their price lists have incentives for their customers if they make a large volume purchase. When buyers buy over a certain dollar amount they get free freight, and when they hit certain higher thresholds—$7,500, for example—distributors offer additional discounts. As a result, retailers and companies have a tendency to place as many orders as possible with one distributor. Distributors are always looking for exclusive deals on "hot" products or services that have strong customer demand because they boost all of their sales.

Retailers

Retailers already buy lots of private-label products, which are typically nonexclusive agreements for a product with a retailer's name on it. A private-label agreement is one option for an OPM deal, but when the retailer makes a three- or four-year commitment (private-label deals typically have no more than a three- to six-month cancellation clause), the retailer is participating as a full-fledged marketing partner. The retailer is also a marketing partner when it agrees to a long-term purchase agreement selling the product under the OPM entrepreneur's brand name. What is important is not the name the product is sold under, but that the retailer has made a long-term purchase commitment.

Service Providers

To understand how service providers can be good marketing partners, consider the example of a large heating and air conditioner service, which is in a great position to promote a new product or another type of service related to heating and air conditioning. If you have a venting and electronic control system to exchange outside air with inside air whenever air gets stale, you could strike a deal with a company that routinely does service work for target customers, and have the company sell your equipment during the service calls. You might also strike a deal with the service company as a marketer, giving the service company a commission every time it sells a whole-house air replacement service that you have another service company provide. For example, you might have a nationwide service contractor, ABC Heating and Air Conditioning, sell the whole-house air exchange service. But that contractor feels that its people are not trained to handle the installation, so you arrange for local installation from a variety of firms throughout the country. You would receive a cut of the profits from every installation done by the local service firms that provided the eventual service.

EMERGENCY RESPONSE

People who act as brokers of services are one existing type of OPM entrepreneur. Shawn Ferguson was an Emergency Medical Technician who observed that many people would prefer a short CPR training course rather than the six- to eight-week course offered by the Red Cross. Ferguson started his business by getting a local community college to offer a short course, which he or his friends taught in return for a share of the revenue. Ferguson then offered the class at a home-health-care show for a small fee. The show promoted the class to attendees, and again Ferguson's friends conducted the class. Ferguson then branched out to become a full-fledged broker, setting up classes at events, trade shows, schools, businesses, and other organizations, and promoting the service to target customers. By this time, he used a group of service providers, who were EMTs working as independent contractors, to provide the training. The profit Ferguson made was the difference between his share of the class revenue and the total fees he paid to the service people who conducted the class.

People Who Sell or Promote to Your Target Customers

As the example of Shawn Ferguson's CPR classes points out, anyone who contacts your target customer in some way is a potential marketer. What counts is that the person has contact with customers, promotes a service, and has the ability to collect revenue. Brokers such as Ferguson can often be found in school fundraising programs. They find services or products that they think parents of children will like and then arrange for the school kids to sell the product, taking their profits as a commission on every dollar of revenue produced from the fundraising program.

FINDING POTENTIAL PARTNERS

Finding partners starts with the target customer. Anyone who is active with your target customer is a potential partner, from associations to local organizations that host an annual festival. Make a list of all the companies and organizations that interact with your targeted customers. The best way to find these companies is by using directories that are posted on Web sites for trade magazines and associations and trade shows. (Later in this chapter, we'll cover how to choose the right partner from among the many possible ones.)

Trade magazines typically have directories that contain a list of manufacturers, manufacturers' representatives, and distributors. Here's an example: I happened to learn that rock salt lamps are popular in Pakistan, both for their soft ambient mood lighting and because when they are lit, the lamps release ions that are believed to have some medicinal value. To look into potential partners, I typed this into the Google search box: *lighting retailer trade magazine*. (I didn't use any quotes, because that would limit my search to sites with those words in that exact order.) At the top of the list that popped up was the site for *Home Lighting and Accessories*, the trade magazine for lighting retailers. The site contained a directory for manufacturers, manufacturers' representatives, and some distributors. I also learned from the magazine that many sales go through manufacturers' reps who set up in merchandise marts, which are showrooms in major centers that retailers visit. I also subscribed to the magazine so I could keep up with the industry. (Most trade magazines are available at no charge or for a low cost.) You can also find trade magazines in Gale's *Directory of Publications and Broadcast Media*, which is available in larger libraries. The listings in Gale's will give you the Web site address to look up on the Internet.

Associations can also be located using Google in exactly the same way as for trade magazines. For the associations related to lighting I found several sources, but the best one was the National Home Furnishings Association. The association's directory for products contained a list of many manufacturers and distributors, and a list of auxiliary members had the names of manufacturers' representatives. Gale's *Encyclopedia of Associations,* also available at libraries, contains a very comprehensive list of associations.

Trade shows are another good source for finding potential partners because most key market suppliers will exhibit at a trade show. Most shows have directories that list all the exhibitors, what their products are, and contact information for each company. Sometimes trade shows will list the exhibitor information on the show's Web site, but often it is incomplete. Your best bet is to just call the trade-show sales office and ask for a copy of last year's directory. You can find the right trade-show contacts in trade magazines and at *www.tsnn.com,* which is a comprehensive Web site directory of both big and small trade shows. You can also find trade show directories at many libraries, or buy a directory at *www.forum123.com.*

WHEN MARKETERS ARE RECEPTIVE TO A DEAL

Marketing partners take on an OPM deal when it helps enhance their overall market presence. For a marketer, the OPM model allows them to strengthen their position quickly with an exciting new product or service, which will then allow them to also make more money from their own internally generated ideas. There are conditions under which an OPM deal is especially attractive to a marketer. The conditions include when:

- New market trends are developing
- The marketer has a significant hole in its product line that needs to be filled
- For whatever reason, the market has lost momentum
- The marketer needs improved margins or improved revenue
- A potential partner has had recent changes in top personnel
- A company doesn't have the resources to introduce a product on its own

Let's consider how each of the above situations can create opportunities for an OPM entrepreneur.

New Market Trends

Downloading music for fees, cell phone conference calls among teenagers, backyard water ponds, Six Sigma supply chain management systems, using eBay as a large-scale marketing outlet, and hybrid golf clubs—these are all new trends in which some companies are winners and others are losers. For an OPM entrepreneur, especially one that is a user of these new products and services, such trends open up opportunities because companies participating in the market don't know for sure what the fast-changing market wants.

Scrapbooking is a good example; that market went from low or no sales to $5 billion in sales in just a few years. Many of the new products in that market came from inventors or others who were diehard scrapbookers; they knew what the market wanted because they were key target customers themselves. People with an interest in scrapbooking and an entrepreneurial urge saw opportunities not only for products, but also for services such as scrapbooking clubs, scrapbook services to record family histories, and scrapbook services for major events. One OPM entrepreneur, for example, organized scrapbooks for weddings, arranging to have the service sold by wedding photographers and the scrapbooks done by a local scrapbook club. The rapidly rising development of combination gourmet kitchen stores and cooking classes is another fast-moving market that is currently opening up market opportunities.

Product Line Gaps

Companies can't afford a hole in their product line, because having multiple sources of supply costs companies money. Most customers will prefer to have just one or two suppliers. This urge to consolidate exists for most businesses, either retail or industrial, and even for consumers. It applies even more to service providers, because companies and consumers both tend to prefer just one supplier.

The urge for customers to consolidate their purchases has dire consequences for marketers with gaps in their product line. They not only lose the sale of the missing item, but they have a hard time getting customers at all. A company won't mind splitting profits on a product that fills a hole in its line, because it believes that filling that hole not only sells the OPM product or service but also provides an enormous lift to the entire product line, which will attract more customers because it is complete.

Lost Momentum

Marketers especially worry when momentum loss is due to new product or service introductions from their competitors. Marketers know that their market momentum is key to their survival. America loves the underdog in sports, but when it comes to buying products and services, they love even more the rising star, the "hot" company in the market. Marketers believe that once you lose your "glamour" status in the market, sales will drop across the entire product line.

Improved Margins

Distributors and retailers might sell a product at a 30 to 40 percent margin. If the distributor commits to a three-year deal for an exclusive selling arrangement, he might receive an additional 5 to 7 percent margin, either as a discount or as a share of the profits. That's a good deal for the retailer. You might wonder whether it is a good deal for the OPM entrepreneur, giving up 5 to 7 percent of the sales price to a retailer that he or she might sell to anyway. The answer is yes—

SUCCESS TIP

Brand building is the key term that marketers use when discussing momentum. Brand building refers to convincing customers and distributors in the market that products or services with the company's brand name on them are a good investment. BMW is a value brand, because people perceive that BMW produces quality products. In general, a strong brand is one for which customers know the product's name and think positively about the product. Dell Computer, for example, has a strong brand name; people know its name and most people feel that the company sells quality products at a competitive price. The more you understand branding, the more effective you can be at selling marketers on the merits of your product. A good starting point for branding is *Building Strong Brands* by David A. Aaker (Free Press, 1996).

if the OPM entrepreneur can't afford to produce the product. The OPM entrepreneur needs a guaranteed sales outlet, or nearly guaranteed outlet, in order to get a provider to invest enough money to launch the concept.

Increased Revenue

Certain functions—such as newsletters, service support, or sponsorships of events—are critical for a marketer to continue in order to keep connected to its customers. But often those activities barely break even in profitability for their companies, and the marketer is looking for ways to create new revenue streams to help offset all of its fixed marketing costs. In a sense, marketing and production are similar, in that they need certain activities to function. A company that wants to market products throughout the country may not be able to afford the sales force needed to do that because it just doesn't have enough revenue. Or the company may not have the resources to put together a promotional program that is strong enough to interest dealers. These companies want to increase their revenue so they will have the resources necessary to perform all the activities expected from a major market supplier.

Change in Top Personnel

New management is always looking to make an impact on their employees and the market. They will go out of their way to look at new ideas and concepts in the hope that they might find an idea that will sell. This situation is especially advantageous for OPM entrepreneurs because they can often get right to the top management people in the company, instead of having to work their way up through lower-level personnel. Trade magazines will list almost all top management personnel changes at most companies in the industry, from small to large. Companies with management changes from one to twelve months old may be receptive to an OPM deal if they feel that the product or service meets a strong market need or desire.

An Inability to Fund Its Own Introduction

Often, a company doesn't have resources to introduce its own ideas. Sometimes the best marketers to approach are small to midsize companies that lack the resources for a major introduction. They might not know how to put together a deal with a manufacturing partner, or might be too busy to go through the work. Look for companies in your market that feature mostly accessories or peripheral equipment or services for other companies. For example, one inventor had the idea of light-absorbing decals that would provide low-level light for six hours in case of a power outage or to provide nightlights for young children and senior citizens. The easiest marketing partners to approach for such an idea are probably specialty lighting manufacturers that sell primarily to small lighting stores. They would like a new product that could help them introduce a line to home improvement stores. Normally these partners wouldn't be able to afford to develop a major new product such as a light-absorbing decal, but the OPM entrepreneur would have arranged with a manufacturer to do the engineering and manufacturing setup, cutting the marketer's cost. A large manufacturer or marketer with lots of money would be able introduce the product on its own, and therefore would be a much harder sell.

CHOOSING THE BEST MARKETING PARTNER

The first key to choosing a potential marketing partner is to remember that OPM stands for *other people's money*. You need to be able to entice someone to put the cash up to make an introduction of a product possible; this is usually the manufacturing or service company provider. These entities won't be interested in putting up the money unless you have a marketing partner that is large enough to potentially sell enough of the product or service to make their investment worthwhile. To choose your target list of potential marketers, follow these steps:

1. *Determine the investment required.* The investment required drives every decision in an OPM deal, because without the investment you can't move forward. Chapter 5 covers finding manufacturers or service providers that can make your product. Those manufacturers will be able to provide you a rough start-up cost estimate. You don't have to obtain a quote from a manufacturer you plan on using; you just need a starting investment point as a reference so you can proceed.

2. *Determine which marketers are capable of delivering annual sales levels fifteen to twenty times the investment.* The manufacturer or service provider will probably want to recover its costs in two years or less. The provider's profit share will probably be about 5 to 10 percent, because the profits will be split three ways. With a 5 percent profit share, the provider would earn 100 percent of its investment back in one year if sales are twenty times the investment.

3. *Discover for which partners your volume will be equivalent to 10 to 25 percent of sales.* Your project should represent a 10 to 25 percent increase in sales to the marketer. If the project is less than 10 percent it will be hard to generate excitement in the marketer, because the project just won't have enough impact. A 10 to 25

percent increase will make a significant difference to both the company's sales totals and its bottom line.

4. *Determine which of the marketers have many characteristics of a company that should be looking for new ideas.* As covered earlier in this chapter, potential targets will need to have several of the characteristics that entice companies to want to make a deal.

5. *Make a judgment about which companies will be easiest to sell.* Any size company can be sold on a concept, but larger marketing partners with branded products are often more difficult to sell. First, they often have a backlog of potential products or services that they could introduce on their own; and second, they typically take time, and sometimes a long time, to make decisions. A large distributor or retailer, or a service provider option, is typically an easier sale, and often a better choice when it can produce significant sales volume.

MARKET REALITY

Marketers will frequently want to know if their commitment will *base load* the manufacturer or service provider, which means that the provider will be investing a substantial sum in new product equipment or even a new plant. This would be in contrast to the OPM concept, which provides *incremental volume.* This term means that the manufacturer makes a modest investment but primarily utilizes existing equipment. You will get two negative reactions from the marketer if it knows that its commitment is considered a base load order. First, the marketer will expect a much lower price.

—continued on next page

TYPES OF DEALS FOR MARKETERS

OPM deals can be set up in a number of ways and you can be flexible when creating the terms of an agreement. Listed below are an array of deal structures that you can suggest to marketers in order to find the one that suits them best. This is just one part of a total OPM deal; you also need a deal structure that keeps you in control (see Chapter 7) and that involves a marketing partner. But you don't want to explain complicated details at this stage of the game. All you need from the marketer is a commitment that is sufficient to convince a provider to invest enough money to move the project forward. These three agreements—a straightforward purchase agreement, purchase agreements with considerations, and private-label agreements—are all easily understood by marketers, and if you can get one from a marketer you can land a provider partner and then work out the more complicated OPM deal structure.

MARKET REALITY

—continued

Traditionally, base load customers receive prices only slightly above cost because the marketer's commitment allows the plant to be built. Second, if the marketer feels it is committing to a base load order, it will be worried that the manufacturer or service provider might not be able to ramp up production fast enough, as production will essentially be on a new line or with a new group of employees. The best answer is usually that the product or service is a variation of the producer's current operations that it will easily be able to handle.

Straightforward Purchase Commitment

The simplest OPM deal is a two- to three-year purchase commitment from one customer that's large enough to entice a manufacturer or service provider to invest. The buyer may not consider itself to be the marketer—you might not have even explained that it is the marketing partner, and it might actually use the product itself if it's an industrial customer—but that doesn't matter. The buyer still provided the order and took the goods. Retailers are a good example of companies that will do this, as are distributors or integrators that buy your product and then include it as a component of their own product. An exhaust system manufacturer, for example, is an integrator who might buy large volumes of an innovative component from an OPM entrepreneur that it will incorporate into its final product.

Firm Purchase Agreements in Return for Considerations

The agreement might call for exclusive rights nationally or in a territory, and for either a short time or for the duration of the agreement. Rather than a total exclusive agreement, the consideration might be that certain features or applications are exclusive to the marketing partner. For example, a chain of surfboard shops might have exclusive rights to a new style of polyurethane wheels on a skateboard, but not exclusive rights to the entire skateboard line.

Agreements may also be entered with price concessions in addition to other considerations. In return for a firm long-term agreement you might have to give up both, and you might also need to offer protected pricing, which you can raise only under certain restricted circumstances.

Private-Label Agreements

A private-label agreement is really no different from the first two options, except that rather than being branded with your name or the service provider's name, the product or service is branded with the marketer's company name. For example, you might offer a service to set up and maintain database systems for a software company named XYZ Database. You have the service provided by service companies throughout the country. In the first two options, the service could be provided by a service company called Database Wizards, with the service still branded with the Database Wizards name, even though XYZ Database would sell the service to its customers. In the private-label example, the service could be named XYZ Off-Site Service Department, with the service branded and sold by the marketing partner, XYZ Database, as if it were its own department.

The deals you might suggest here can typically be handled by a purchase order or straight buy-and-sell agreement. Don't promise the marketer that the final agreement will be that simple; tell the marketer you simply need this commitment in order to entice a provider company to put up the money or produce the produce or service. Web sites with simple sample forms that you can utilize for a buy-and-sell or private-label agreement include *www.allbusiness.com* (my top choice); *www.legalforms.com; www.findlegalforms.com; www.lawdepot.com; www.americalawyer.com;* and *www.findlaw.com.*

LANDING AN INSIDE CONTACT

As mentioned earlier, OPM deals are easier to strike and move faster when there is a strong supporter inside the potential partner company. You want to find the supporter early, before you make any formal sales calls. The contact can then help you fine-tune your presentations to the company's needs. She will also advocate for your project inside the company, urging management to move ahead with your offer. Typically you want to find either a regional manager or a marketing manager to help you.

You don't need to go with your hat in your hand when working with an inside contact, because the contact actually gains as much as you do when presenting the project; in fact, it is a win-win situation for the contact. If the inside contact brings the project to the company and the company successfully introduces the concept, she looks like a real go-getter who is helping the company advance. If the project doesn't go through, the contact still looks like a go-getter, an image that will help her at some point. The following steps will usually get you an inside contact with a potential partner company:

1. *Start with a salesperson.* We discussed in Chapter 1 how to meet salespeople by requesting literature and attending association meetings. You can also meet salespeople just by walking up and talking to them in their booth. Try to walk the shows early in the morning or late in the afternoon, when the number of real customers is low. Once you meet salespeople, ask to take them to lunch because you need some input from them on a concept you think might work in the market.

2. *Use the initial presentation that you prepared to explain your concept and the research you've put into the project.* Don't try to sell the salesperson; just show her the presentation with the observation that you're trying to decide what would be a good next step.

3. *Ask for her input on your idea and what could be done to make the concept go.* The salesperson might ask for more detailed information in which case you can ask her to sign a Non-Disclosure Agreement (see Appendix B for an example). Be receptive to what she has to say, then ask if this is a concept that her company might be interested in. More than likely the person will have quite a few comments about how it could be done, with suggestions for making the concept "just right" for the target company.

4. *Arrange to meet regional or marketing managers.* If the salesperson is on board, make at least some of the changes she suggested, and then ask the salesperson if she could set up a meeting with the regional or marketing manager. Usually that person can meet with you, either when the manager comes to town, or at a trade show, or you might be able to visit the company's location.

5. *Use your contacts to help set up the presentation.* Once you convey your concept to the regional or marketing manager, that person will be able to set up a key meeting with the right people at the company. Often the manager will introduce you and give a little sales pitch about how your concept could have a significant impact on the company before you even get started.

If the salesperson or regional manager doesn't want to go forward, find out what that person didn't like about your concept. You may have problems with the concept that can easily be remedied, and then you can try again.

THE FINAL SELECTION

After investigating a number of possibilities, you should select three or four candidates to be marketing partners. For each one, fill out the following scorecard. Rate each characteristic 1 to 5, with 5 being the highest rating. Select the marketer with the highest score as your prime target.

MARKETER SCORECARD

Marketer's Name:	Rate from 1 (low) to 5 (high)
Capable of generating sales twenty times the investment required	
Project represents a 10 to 25 percent increase in its sales	
Established, strong market position	
Inside contact(s) established	
Needs to reestablish market momentum	
Recent change in top personnel	
Willingness to sign confidential agreements	
Total Score:	

FIVE

FUND PRODUCTION: LOCATING PROVIDERS WILLING TO INVEST

Providers are looking for opportunities, and they will therefore offer a quote on most jobs. But an OPM entrepreneur has several constraints that make the task of finding the right provider a formidable challenge. Providers must front most of the money (which for some projects is considerable), offer pricing that provides enough margin for everyone to make money, and be able to produce enough to satisfy the marketer. Last, but hardly least, your provider has to be quality conscious, and the product or service must be right each and every time, or the marketer could drop the project in a big hurry.

Not every provider is going to meet these requirements. Providers, as a rule, will only be willing to make a deal if they have an underutilized plant or service staff, or if they need more volume to overcome the burden of their fixed costs. The ideal product provider will have all the right tooling and equipment in place to produce your product, and the ideal service provider will have the right staff, training, and service capabilities. The manufacturer can be in the United States or overseas, since many foreign manufacturers will now fund products for which they can be guaranteed sales. You have to be careful to check out the providers closely and get firm commitments from them, because the biggest risk in any project is that the manufacturer or service provider will pull out.

In this chapter, you'll learn how to better understand the manufacturing and service provider world, which is one that most readers will be experiencing for the first time. You'll then be provided with a step-by-step plan to follow to select a provider. This chapter will:

- Explain how manufacturers or service providers view a potential OPM deal and when they will respond with a yes
- Show you how to find potential manufacturers and service providers who have the right equipment and staff and are in the right situation to potentially fund a project
- Explain the steps to take so the provider is mentally ready for your offer
- Illustrate how to set a firm price-point target to give to a manufacturer or service provider
- Offer a list of questions you need to have answered by potential manufacturers or service providers
- Provide a checklist for determining which manufacturer or service provider to select

NOTHING IS IMPOSSIBLE

Jon Parker grew enthralled in his twenties with wines and, when he was selling robotic equipment in California, with the process of developing wine. But the market seemed tough to break into, with large investments needed for both land and production equipment. Even so, Parker wanted to make his own distinctive Chardonnay and Merlot. Parker sampled hundreds of existing wines to determine the mix of qualities he felt were missing in the market and then set out to find a way to become a winemaker.

Parker didn't have the money to start his own winery. He felt, though, that he could get the support of distributors in Ohio, Indiana, Illinois, and Michigan (the region around his Indiana hometown) as well as in California (where he had been working for five years) if he could create wines with their own distinctive flavor. His next step, funded by investors, was to hire an international vintner. The vintner determined what taste Parker was looking for by writing down Parker's comments as he tasted dozens of wines. With that data, the vintner was able to develop wines that Parker felt provided a distinctive taste in the market. Parker was then able to get a California wine producer to grow the grapes and produce the vintner's wine formula. Sales took off with the distributors, and sales were expanded from the original five-state area after just three years. Everyone was a winner. Parker bought from the winery and sold to the distributor, with his only investment being the money he paid the vintner.

HOW PROVIDERS RESPOND TO AN OPM DEAL

The ideal situation for a provider is having guaranteed contracts on its own branded products and services, with high margins. A second choice would be a long-term production contract with an established marketer, who pays for all costs and still produces a significant profit for the provider. An OPM deal provides a long-term commitment for volume, but it does so with a profit-sharing arrangement, and it typically requires the provider to put up the funds to introduce the concept. An OPM deal is a long way off from what providers consider their top choice for new business. Fortunately for you, providers don't always have access to their top choices, and then the OPM deal becomes an attractive offer to them. Because an OPM deal isn't the first choice, you face three ramifications: most providers will initially push for a deal highly favorable to their side; not every provider will be interested; and you will have to do research to know which providers are the best candidates to accept a deal.

Since an OPM deal is the providers' fourth or fifth choice, you have to expect them to push for a deal that's more favorable to them, with their preferred choice being for you to give them a guaranteed contract and pay all costs. You might need to go back and forth with providers several times over several months before they agree, and they will often agree only when they believe there is no other way to introduce the concept. The next section of this chapter deals with positioning a provider so it will accept an OPM deal even if that deal isn't its first choice.

Providers that are reasonably profitable and running fairly close to their capacity are probably not good candidates. They are likely to be reasonably profitable if they are running at 80 percent or higher capacity. Those providers will still want to add business but will probably be a tough sell for you, because they may think your deal is unattractive and will want instead to wait for a full-priced deal from a well-funded customer.

You can fairly easily conduct research to find the providers who will be good candidates. Knowing which provider candidates might approve an OPM deal is essential, or you will waste too much time negotiating with the wrong companies. Your research strategy should include talking with suppliers in the market, checking available financial data, and asking questions and requesting quotes to reveal the provider's situation. These topics will be covered in the upcoming sections in this chapter. The conditions under which a provider will be open to an OPM deal include the following:

1. *The provider is operating below 70 percent capacity.* In this case it may be at or below its break-even production point. It needs more volume to become profitable.

2. *The provider has only short-term orders.* OPM deals typically promise two to three years of orders, which offers stability to the manufacturer.

3. *The company is looking to grow.* New business, if it is guaranteed, is still a vehicle for growth even if the provider has a lower profit percentage.

4. *The company is facing competition with lower costs.* Extra production that doesn't require large fixed costs will cut the costs of a provider's entire product line. The old adage is true: as volume goes up, price goes down.

5. *The provider has the right equipment and staff in place.* The provider's investment is modest if it has the right equipment, making it much easier for the provider to move ahead.

6. *The provider has the financial capability to add a new product or service.* You need a creditworthy partner; you can usually find out information about a company's creditworthiness at *www. smallbusiness.dnb.com.*

FINDING POTENTIAL PROVIDERS

You have four tasks when locating a manufacturer or service provider: discovering what type of company could produce your concept, locating specific manufacturers or providers with the right type of staff and equipment for your concept, discovering which providers need more volume, and determining which providers are in the right size range for your project.

For example, Jon Parker, the wine entrepreneur mentioned earlier in the chapter, had to take the following steps:

1. Figure out the set of conditions, or the wine valley, that could produce his grapes (the type of company that could create the product).

2. Locate in that valley the companies that had the right type of equipment to produce his style of wine.

3. Discover which companies needed additional production.

4. Finally, determine which potential providers had a volume level that was a good fit for his expected wine production.

THE RIGHT TYPE OF COMPANY

Should a new style of barbecue grill be made with punching and forming, rotational molding, or machining? Should a service that provides inventory control for just-in-time inventory shipments come from a software company, a data storage company with software capabilities, or an Internet service provider (ISP) with more extensive interactive programming capabilities? You might have trouble figuring out just what type of companies to even approach to be your provider. If you don't know the type of company that provides your product or service, contact your local office of SCORE (Service Corps of Retired Executives); you can find the location at *www.score.org*. SCORE has many retired executives at every local office, and one area they are very strong in is identifying what types of companies will provide the service or product you want to produce.

If you have a product, and SCORE can't help, go to local prototype shops, which you can find in the yellow pages or by doing a search on Google. Ask for a prototype quote on your product, and ask the shop what type of manufacturer would have the equipment required to produce the product. For service providers, look at several trade magazines, start calling companies that seem to offer services that seem close to what you want, and ask if they can produce your service. If they can't do the job, ask what type of company could. Typically, you can find what type of companies you want to work with after just three or four calls.

In the past, many more OPM deals seemed to involve products rather than services. But that is starting to shift drastically. Service Upgrades is a sales organization set up exclusively to sell and market service and maintenance contracts for high-technology companies. The company was started when its founders discovered that companies were only realizing about 80 percent of their total potential service revenue. Eighty percent seems high, but in a $60 billion industry it still means there is a revenue gap in excess of $10 billion. Service Upgrades decided to pursue this opportunity. It started out by signing up several high-tech companies, promising only that it would figure out how to increase the companies' service revenue. The organization agreed with its clients that it would only be paid a commission on any revenue it produced.

Service Upgrades then started going out to its clients' customers to find out why they weren't buying as much service as its clients' service revenue models indicated they should be buying. Service Upgrades found that, in many cases, its clients just didn't have their services configured in a way that met its customers' needs. Service Upgrades then had its clients add services that the customers wanted, or provide services in a different format to generate the extra income its clients wanted.

Service Upgrades was operating in the OPM arena, but in a slightly different way. Its service providers were its technology clients. The service providers were also the companies who had the need—increased service revenue—that Service Upgrades was meeting. Service Upgrades could have found a marketing partner then, but chose instead to do the marketing on its own. It was able to raise $6 million to fund its marketing activities rather than hire a marketing company.

FINDING READY-TO-GO PROVIDERS

The easiest way to locate providers with the right equipment is to talk to their suppliers. For example, you might have an idea to provide a service that will automatically signal a parent when his or her child is accessing dangerous Internet sites or exchanging questionable e-mails. The service works with a monitoring software package that sends a cell phone signal to a service provider when questionable activities occur. The service provider then verifies that the warning is warranted, disables the Internet connection, and notifies the parent. The service provider needs telephone switching equipment to perform this service. An OPM entrepreneur simply needs to call up the right type of telephone switching suppliers (which he can determine from the trade magazine for telecommunications equipment or through a SCORE counselor) and ask which companies involved in the Internet service have that type of telecommunications equipment.

This procedure is typically easier with manufacturing equipment because there are distributors who sell equipment from a variety of suppliers and are often well connected with all the suppliers in their market. For example, in Minneapolis, where I live, Galaxy Plastics distributes injection-molding plastics equipment for ten manufacturers. I can call up a salesperson and simply tell him I'm looking for a manufacturer with a certain type of equipment. The salesperson always gives me at least a few names.

You should still go through the same procedure if it looks like you need to go overseas to find a manufacturer to cut costs. Knowing which North American companies are the right fit gives you the information you need to tell a consulate or sourcing agent to find the right overseas supplier. An excellent site for global manufacturers is *www.GlobalSources.com*. Also check out the sites *www.mfgquote.com*, *www.outsourceking.com*, and *www.ec21.com* for help getting overseas quotes.

PROVIDERS THAT NEED MORE VOLUME

Your next step is to determine who needs to increase production of either products or services. You can use the same contacts you used to find the candidates with the right equipment. Simply say to them, "I'm working on a project with very tight margins that probably won't be of interest to a company that is running at fairly full capacity. Do you know companies that need volume that are likely to meet my margin requirements?" Salespeople and regional managers to the industry typically know the situation for most of their customers and can generally steer you to several suppliers that could be potential providers for your OPM deal.

If most suppliers of your type of product are overseas, you will need to get a list of manufacturers and just start by asking for quotes on your product from seven or eight suppliers. The ones that respond with the best quotes are probably going to be the best candidates.

THE RIGHT VOLUME RANGE

You want to check the sales volume of those candidates you've identified to find ones for which the potential volume you represent is 10 to 35 percent of current volume. If your volume is

OPM ENTREPRENEUR RESOURCES

Most business research books are written for big companies and are not very helpful for the individual entrepreneur. One book that successfully bucks this trend is *Successful Business Research: Where Do I Get the Numbers?* by Rhonda Abrams and Veronica Adams (Planning Shop, 2005). This helpful book, which is paired with a CD, guides you through the online research process, including how to find Internet sites with (usually free) data and how to interpret and use the data you find. It's the book to have if you run into trouble finding the research data you need.

less than 10 percent of a company's volume, your project won't make enough impact on the company to make it worth its while to proceed with an OPM deal. If the volume is more than 35 percent, you will need to worry about whether the company can actually produce enough product. You can find information regarding companies' sizes at *www.business.com*, *www.hoovers.com*, *www.smallbusiness.dnb.com*, and *www.knowx.com*.

APPROACHING PROVIDERS

Manufacturers or service providers are used to people contracting for their services and paying the bills. They might have to amortize start-up costs (which means that buyers pay for start-up costs and then recover those costs with a per-unit charge on each part produced or service rendered until the total costs are paid). When you approach potential providers, they will always want to start conversations by requesting that you pay all the costs. Providers might just walk away if you immediately try to switch them over to accepting an OPM approach. You want to move them over more slowly by having the conversation in stages, from paying for the costs to asking the provider to absorb most of the up-front costs.

You are not misleading your potential provider because, for the most part, what is good for the provider is also good for you. Paying the money in a traditional fashion is more profitable for an entrepreneur than is an OPM arrangement. If you find a marketer to sell your product or service, you might be better off financially if you can get an investor to put up the money for production, because you then won't need to share as much of the profit stream with the manufacturer or service provider. If the deal develops as promisingly as you expect, you may pay the costs yourself, or, if you can't afford that, find investors to pay the costs. The steps for approaching a manufacturer or provider follow the steps that also could financially benefit you the most—investing in your production and buying and selling the product or service yourself or through a typical distribution channel.

1. *Ask for a quote from the provider.* Tell the provider that you have come up with an exciting new concept, that you have found a marketing partner that potentially wants to sell the product, and that you need a quote to put together your business plan. Tell the provider that you plan on having the concept, product, or service outsourced rather than making or providing the service yourself. Ask for a quote for the volumes you will need.

2. *Request that the provider meet the marketer's price.* Wait a few weeks and then tell the manufacturer you need to meet a certain price to make the project go (the next section in this chapter explains how to determine the price point to request). Explain that your research and the marketing partner both indicate that the projected price is too high for the product to sell, and that you and the partner feel that you can't continue unless you hit the targeted price point.

3. *Ask clarifying questions.* There will always be some questions about the quote—for instance, questions about packaging costs, responsibility for certain expenses, insurance coverage, and other items. After a few weeks, go back and clarify those items. If you are having trouble finding questions, just ask a consultant from SCORE (*www.score.org*), or go to the local Small Business Development Center (find the nearest location at *www.sba.gov/sbdc*) and ask a consultant to help you review the price quote to find out whether there are any items that aren't clear.

4. *Ask for a quote base with amortized start-up costs.* Tell the provider you can share the marketing company's name, its sales

, and even a contact as long as your provider contact signs either a Non-Disclosure Agreement or a Mutual Confidentiality Agreement. Amortizing start-up costs is a common request, and in some cases, especially if you get the manufacturer to wait for payment until you get paid, it is a full OPM deal.

5. *Bring up the OPM concept.* After waiting at least a few weeks, you can bring up the OPM concept to the provider, with the provider paying start-up costs in return for a bigger share of the profits in a project that will be promoted by both you and your marketing partner.

Don't become so enamored of the OPM concept that you forget that your goal is to make the best deal possible for you. As you walk down these steps for negotiating with the manufacturer, you may find that you can execute one of the earlier steps, either because the provider is offering favorable terms or because you can get a bank loan or investor to cover the costs. If you can do that, you might make more money with little or no additional risk.

SET A TARGETED PRICE POINT

If you ask manufacturers or service providers for a price, they will typically come back with a price that provides plenty of profit for them. But your product or service is going to have to be cost competitive, you are going to have to pay a marketing company 20 to 25 percent of the sales revenue for its efforts and expenses, and you need to make some money too. If the price is too high, the deal will just fall through. You need to work in reverse and determine the price you need from the provider for the project to make enough money to pay all the partners, and then ask the provider to meet that price. Here's how:

1. *Start by using the price that you have determined is an ideal selling price.* This figure will be based on your market research and your discussions with industry people and potential marketing partners. (See Chapter 3, pages 43–45.)

2. *Determine the dollars the marketing partner will receive.* You have a suggested retail price from consumers, but the marketer will receive less than that if the product is sold through retailers or a distribution channel. Distribution channel discounts vary by market and industry, but you can get the right dollar amount by asking your contact what price his company needs to charge for a product or service to be sold at a given price. For example, ask, "If the suggested retail price is $49.95, what price would you charge your distributors?"

3. *Deduct marketing company charges.* Marketing partners will typically want a profit of 10 percent of their actual sales dollars over and above their marketing and sales costs. Their typical sales costs are 5 to 10 percent of sales, so you are looking at a 15 to 20 percent cut of the sales volume going to the marketer. This is not 10 to 15 percent of the end-user price, but of the price the marketer receives. Determining the price up to this point might look like the following table:

Price Point	Price	Comment
End-user price	$15.00	Set by market research
Retailer price	$9.00	Purchases at 40% off retail
After marketer's share	$7.20	20% of the marketer's price to the retailer

4. *Deduct an OPM entrepreneur fee.* You want to make as much as possible, but certainly no less than 5 percent of the money left after the marketer's share. I recommend that you set your share at

10 percent of the price to the distribution channel, which in the example in the table above would be ninety cents. You may need to adjust the percentage if the providers can't meet the targeted price.

5. *Tell the provider the targeted price.* This is the end-user price as determined by your research less all the other discounts or profit sharing listed in the first four steps. Always ask for a price before telling the provider the price you need to hit, just in case the provider's price is less than the targeted price you establish in this process.

QUESTIONS TO ASK

You should by now have several manufacturers to choose from—at least that's what you hope for. Your goal now is to package the provider's capability so that the marketer will be willing to move ahead. The provider partner's ability to deliver a quality product or service is essential to obtaining a commitment from the marketer. Pose the following questions to manufacturers you are seriously considering. You will obtain information that your marketing partner will probably ask you about, and it will help you to determine which provider will be able to move ahead.

OPM ENTREPRENEUR RESOURCES

Pricing on value, rather than going for a low price, is an issue most OPM entrepreneurs will need to raise with their partners. You need a price level based on value, because you need to have a high-profit sale to pay all the partners. An excellent resource for determining a high-value proposition for your concept is *Value Added Selling: How to Sell More Profitably, Confidently, and Professionally by Competing on Value, Not Price* by Tom Reilly (2nd edition, McGraw-Hill, 2002). Also check out *The Strategy and Tactics of Pricing: A Guide to Profitable Decision Making* by Thomas T. Nagle and Reed K. Holden (3rd edition, Prentice-Hall, 2005).

1. *What volume, either manufacturing or service, can the provider produce without a significant investment?* Comment: Ideally the company's investment requirement to start production will be low.

2. *What investment is needed to reach the next plateau of volume without a major expansion?* Comment: You need to ensure that the company is able to grow production at least 50 percent without a major, costly expansion, because the company might be reluctant to make an investment that big for a lower-profit OPM deal.

3. *What is the highest quality standard the provider achieves? For what type of product or service does it achieve that quality?* Comment: You want to be sure that the marketer and provider deal in similar quality standards. A marketer of high-quality goods will not want to switch gears to products produced with lower quality standards.

4. *What is the provider's current lead time, both for the first order and then for subsequent orders?* Comment: Typically, short lead times for both the first order and subsequent orders indicate that the provider needs your business.

5. *How much of the product or service will be produced in-house versus outsourced?* Comment: Providers will be much more willing to agree to an OPM deal if most of the production or service is in-house, because in-house production is typically more profitable.

6. *What type of product liability insurance does the provider have? Would its liability insurance cover your concept?* Comment: You may need product liability insurance too, even if the manufacturer has it. If the provider's insurance covers your concept, you

may be able to inexpensively be added on as a rider to its policy. If the manufacturer doesn't have insurance that covers your concept, it could require a significant up-front fee, sometimes as high as $25,000.

7. *What type of concessions will the provider make for a two- to three-year contract commitment?* Comment: Manufacturers needing production will offer more concessions than will those who are running at a high production rate.

8. *What type of support staff does the provider have for correcting problems in the factory as well as those that occur in the field?* Comment: There *will* be problems, and you need a quick response to correct those problems or your project could lose all of its momentum.

9. *Does the manufacturer have other branded products that it sells on its own?* Comment: Companies will always support their branded products first. Companies that have more than 50 percent of their production in their branded products might drop out if their branded products start selling better.

10. *Does the provider have other commitments for the equipment it will use on your product? If the equipment is shared, how can you be guaranteed that you won't face a shortfall in production?* Comment: In a crunch, the provider will produce what it makes the most money on; you could be out in the cold if the equipment is used for too many projects.

11. *What type of overhead rate would be included in the price? Is that the company's standard overhead rate?* Comment: Overhead rate is a reflection of the amount of fixed costs that a company has, and to a lesser degree how much volume is going through the plant. A high overhead rate could mean that the

company's fixed costs are too high, which is bad for you, or it could mean that production is low, which means the company needs your business and is a good OPM candidate.

12. *How does your overhead rate compare to the industry average? If higher, why is that?* Comment: If the company has a high overhead rate that is due to lack of production, it will tell you that, and then state that it is taking a low profit on your business so you are not penalized by the overhead rate.

13. *Is there a volume level where that overhead rate would drop?* Comment: Companies with fairly full production normally won't change the overhead rate if volume goes up, because they feel they could get other production if they didn't take your order. Companies who need production will drop the overhead charge, sometimes two or more times at increasing volume levels.

MARKET REALITY

Overhead absorption will be the determining factor in most providers' decisions. Overhead refers to a company's fixed costs such as rent, insurance, maintenance, information technology (IT) services, and salaries for certain employees such as quality control engineers, dispatchers, schedulers, and purchasing agents. Companies determine a product's or service's total cost based on actual cost to produce the product or service plus a percentage of the company's overhead costs. Overhead charges range by industry, but they can be 30 to 50 percent of the overall costs of a product or service. When a producer of goods or services adds new production, the increase allows the overhead to be spread over more goods or services, and the overhead charge of each item or service goes down.

—continued on next page

14. *Is the company equipped to handle packaging as well as delivery direct to end users?* Comment: You want to avoid taking actual possession of the product, because that will significantly raise your costs and capital requirements. The provider needs to handle all aspects of packaging or delivery for a deal to succeed.

15. *Is the company's credit line large enough to handle the volume you project? If not, what volume can it support?* Comment: You need the provider to have the financial capability to meet both your current and future production needs.

MARKET REALITY
—continued

This means that an OPM deal allows the provider partner to cut costs on all the products it is currently producing, and it makes money not just on the production generated by an OPM deal, but also on the reduced overhead costs on its current production, thereby allowing the provider to either make more money on that production, or to bid more competitively on other jobs. This decrease in costs can be substantial. If overhead charges are 40 percent of the total product or service costs, a 25 percent increase in production will drop a company's cost per unit by 10 percent.

THE FINAL SELECTION

You should now be able to select three to four provider candidates that appear to meet your requirements. Rate each candidate from one to five on the characteristics in the following scorecard, with five being the highest rating. Select the providers with the highest score as your prime targets.

Provider's Name:	Rate from 1 (low) to 5 (high)
Capacity below 70 percent	
Right equipment in place	
Financially able to support deal	
Volume fit for expected sales	
Offered short lead time	
Willing to adjust price with increased production	
Willing to amortize start-up costs	
Able to meet the targeted price	
Able to double production	
Adequate liability insurance	
Willing to prioritize OPM production	
Total Score:	

SIX

FURTHER RESEARCH: SIGN A LETTER OF INTENT AND HAVE PARTNERS PAY

Your initial presentations might have potential partners excited about your deal, but when pressed to sign an agreement they could back off. They might tell you they want more research, or they might waffle and not say what the problem is, but in either case you may need to offer some additional market testing to show that the product will sell. This might require producing prototypes or a small production run; taking products to a trade show to gauge end-user and distribution response; running consumer or distribution focus groups; selling products at a major store; attempting to sell services to a target group of potential customers; or going out to end users and getting direct feedback. There are costs for this testing, and if the partners like the project, they will typically pay or split the expenses. The partners might not pay if the costs are high, but they will almost always pay if the costs are small compared to the costs to launch the project.

Many first-time OPM entrepreneurs will consider further research a nuisance. Actually, it can help to encourage partners to sign a Letter of Intent (LOI), which is the first agreement in proceeding to a final agreement, and which also can help to make partners feel more confident that your deal is in their best interest. Instead of jumping from some initial conversations into a final agreement, you will find it easier instead to have companies sign up on a more gradual basis; this allows them to become acclimated to the idea of working with you and another OPM partner. An LOI simply states that a company is interested in the project, is willing to work with the partners to better understand the concept's market potential, and intends to enter into a formal arrangement if the testing is successful. Getting an LOI signed is a strategic moment for you because it is a significant step to a final agreement. It is also a step that is fairly easy to execute because the partner is only committing to further investigate your idea with a requirement of, ideally, only a modest investment.

In this chapter, we'll explore one common way to get partner companies to make a small commitment to the OPM entrepreneur's project. You'll be provided with a framework for structuring an LOI and the subsequent testing program so that partners will commit to the initial stages of the project. This chapter will:

- Discuss why testing provides an easy entry platform for partner companies
- Explain what an LOI is and how to ask partners to sign one
- Show the power of a promise of a full financial analysis
- Provide a list of the best types of testing programs
- Show how to develop a testing plan that meets everyone's needs
- Suggest approaches for getting commitments about what each company will do next if test results are positive
- Provide a timetable and a budget to use to set up the testing
- Show how to approach partners so they will pay for the project
- Explain that corrective action may be needed but that, most of the time, it won't present a problem

Sandra Rycroft was a dedicated scrapbook enthusiast. She often used die cuts (a picture or object shaped or formed as if cut out by scissors—for example, a picture of a football that is shaped like a football) as decorations on her pages. But after a while she got tired of using standard die cuts that anyone could use and longed for her own unique images. Her husband had some mechanical aptitude, and he was able to create a small cutting roller that did a job that was barely acceptable, but that also showed that the concept worked.

Rycroft then struck up a conversation with the local sales representative for one of the three largest scrapbook distributors, whose company supplied equipment to virtually every scrapbook retailer. She set up a meeting, and the salesperson thought the idea would be a big winner if its operational rough spots could be smoothed out. Rycroft wasn't able to find a local manufacturer to help her produce a better prototype, but a local sourcing agent for Taiwan found a supplier there that would work on the product and would sign a confidentiality agreement. The manufacturer agreed to do the advanced prototype at no charge, in return for a letter stating that Rycroft would give the business to the manufacturer provided she could get a tangible commitment from the distributor.

Rycroft told the salesperson her situation, and he arranged for a meeting with a marketing manager at a convention two months later. The distributor signed a letter of intent with Rycroft, and the manufacturer went ahead and worked to develop the prototype, which required four iterations before it was "market ready." Rycroft ended up getting a commission on all products that the Taiwanese manufacturer sold to the distributor.

AN EASY ENTRY PLATFORM

You succeed in moving forward with an OPM concept when potential partners are convinced that your concept has large growth and profit potential. The key point in that statement is that companies must be convinced. You can talk all you want, but that won't necessarily sell a company on your concept's merits. When you first present a concept, you never want to leave the meeting with the company's only commitment being that it will think things over. Instead you should ask, "What steps could I take that would satisfy you that the product can be a big market winner?"

This question shifts the decision-making matrix for the company from a difficult decision—signing an OPM deal—to a much easier decision: Should we investigate the idea further? If companies suggest further development work, ask, "Does this project look like it has promise to you, or are you just pushing off the decision to say no? Please let me know if you are not interested so I can pursue someone else."

Further research or development gives your decision-maker an easier path to follow, but it also is a step that allows your project to generate support from people within a company, because they can follow the project during a development phase, when the risk to the company is low. You are better off, of course, if partners will sign an agreement without any further testing or development, but don't be upset if you need further work; that probably happens in at least 50 percent of OPM deals.

USING LOIs

LOIs, and a similar type of agreement called Memorandums of Understanding (MOU), are agreements that are commonly used when companies are interested in working in a partnership relationship of some sort. In my experience, LOIs are better because they can be less complicated than can MOUs. To succeed in starting the agreement process, you need to understand what an LOI is, why it is useful, and how to present one to a company.

Appendix B includes a sample LOI. If you aren't familiar with Letters of Intent, you might want to read the one in the Appendix before continuing on with this section. An LOI does the following:

- It explains that the parties are working toward an agreement to work together to introduce a concept.
- It states that the parties will sign a formal agreement if they decide to move ahead.
- It lists the steps the potential partners will take prior to signing an agreement.

An LOI is not binding and doesn't commit a company to moving forward into a final agreement. Rather, it is an expression by a potential partner that it is interested in pursuing a project and potentially signing a deal.

You want to sign an LOI with potential partners because it lessens the odds that either partner will just take your idea and proceed without you. You may sign a non-disclosure statement or mutual confidentiality form with companies, but those agreements have a glaring weakness: companies are released from their confidentiality if the concept you share with them becomes known from another source. If another person has thought of the concept, or if the information in the market that led you to your concept becomes available, the company may no longer be obligated to keep your idea secret. An LOI adds to the confidentiality, stating that the company's intent is to investigate your concept with the intent of forming an agreement to introduce the product. That adds reinforcement to your confidentiality agreement, and I've found that companies will generally honor their LOIs.

Often companies will claim that a confidentiality agreement is sufficient. An OPM deal provides an ideal structure for asking companies to sign an LOI in addition to a Mutual Confidentiality Agreement. You can tell the marketing partner that the provider won't invest in the research phase unless it has a formal commitment from the marketing partner. You can take the same tack with the provider company, saying the marketing company won't move ahead without a formal commitment from the provider. Both companies will also want to know who the other company is so they can research its capabilities. Once companies sign an LOI you can tell them who the other partner is, and arrange for a meeting between the partners if that's desired. You should prepare the initial draft of the LOI to be sure it isn't too complicated. Expect the companies to take a minimum of two weeks to have the document reviewed and approved.

MARKET SHIFTS DELIVER OPPORTUNITIES

Steve Harland was a sourcing agent who helped marketers and manufacturers find low-cost offshore production. One of his problems was that his customers had trouble finding financing for the operating capital to run their businesses. The cause of the problem was that the companies frequently operated as limited liability companies (LLCs), and they had few assets except the inventory they brought in from overseas. Banks were leery of loaning them money because the companies didn't have collateral.

At a party, Harland overheard someone lamenting that investment opportunities were grim in 2005. The stock market was declining, returns on bonds were too low, and the investor felt that the housing market might be on a bubble. Steve suggested to the potential investor that a new opportunity existed, providing operating capital financing for companies with limited assets that were bringing in large overseas shipments. The investor was interested but thought that Harland's sourcing business was too small to justify setting up a financing group.

Harland then rounded up a much larger sourcing group, Telecom Sourcing, as a marketing partner. The group had more customers and brought in higher-value parts than Harland did. That group also provided inventory, shipping, and billing services for its customers. Telecom Sourcing felt that adding short-term operation financing for shipments was a natural extension of its services.

But the investor group was worried that the inventory could be sold by its client without the client repaying the loan. The investor group was also uncertain about the legal costs of setting up a company to finance operational capital needs. Telecom Sourcing solved the first problem by holding shipments until the repayment was agreed to by the client and investor group. The legal costs were up in the air, however, and Telecom Sourcing had its own concerns about whether or not its clients would want the service. The companies had interest but also had concerns, so they signed LOIs in order to conduct research while keeping the project alive.

The deal went through only after the partners conducted enough research to satisfy their concerns. Without a research phase, Harland probably would never have had a deal. Harland now plays a key role as the marketing specialist on financing for Telecom Solutions and receives a small take on all the financing his concept generates. Telecom Solutions doesn't receive anything on the financing but benefits from increased revenue by storing and shipping its customers' goods.

THE IMPORTANCE OF A FULL FINANCIAL ANALYSIS

Another common reason that companies won't sign a deal is that there isn't a financial analysis, which would show that the concept will produce sufficient profits to share with all the partners. Your potential partners' marketing and sales departments might be ready go forward if you develop more end-user and distribution channel data, but that doesn't mean the company will be ready to go. Often projects need to be signed off by the finance department. This will typically require a financial analysis. Always ask your partners if their companies will require a financial analysis before moving forward. If they will, you need to be sure your research pulls together the facts an accountant will need. Ask for a contact from each company to help you generate the numbers you need for an analysis:

- Sales forecast for three years
- Price
- Projected production costs
- Projected start-up costs
- Expected marketing costs
- Projected service and maintenance costs

BEST RESEARCH/DEVELOPMENT PROGRAMS

The research or development programs that you present should show that the path to success is clear. You are better off suggesting a fairly comprehensive testing program that answers all doubts, even though it takes longer and costs more, because companies will be leery of loose ends. Let your partners suggest that your testing program is too comprehensive and ask that you go with a simpler program.

Product or Service Development

You can't be sure that the project is right until the final product or service is complete and tested. There are several common steps you can offer that will address the product or service questions:

1. Produce a final production unit or full-service procedure for an internal check on performance.

2. Prepare a final engineering or service protocol package to determine accurate costs.

3. Prepare a run of five or six products that can be sent out for end-user testing.

4. Train three or four service or salespeople in the new concept and then have them present the comments to potential customers.

Market Testing

There is no limit to the market testing that you can do. Because a quick introduction is appealing to OPM partners, you want to concentrate on testing that can be quickly completed but still proves that the product will sell. You want end users to prove to partners that you have the right product. The methods you can suggest should include both testing for product reliability, or the service's ability to meet the customers' goals, and market testing that shows that customers want and will buy the product. For example:

1. End-user testing for function. Products can be given to or services can be performed for customers, and the customers' experience can be evaluated.

2. Laboratory tests on products can be conducted for reliability and safety.

3. A review by top experts or market influencers can be conducted for both products and services.

4. Products or services can be presented to ten customers, or five people in the distribution channel, in order to gauge the market's response.

5. The concept can be presented at trade shows, either in a booth or with a presentation to a large group of attendees, to determine the concept's appeal.

6. A market test in a geographic area or for a specific application can be conducted by actually selling the product or service to a segment of the market.

7. Focus groups can be conducted with users or retailers with the finished product versus competitive products or services.

DEVELOP A TESTING PLAN

You will want to keep control of the research process for two reasons: first, because by being in control you can expedite the process; and second, because controlling research and development, even if you don't do the work, helps you have a degree of control in the final agreement. The best way to keep control is to take the initiative with the plan, compile the initial action list on your own, and then obtain acceptance for the plan from the partners. The steps to take are to obtain input from partners; prepare a list of options; have the partners select options to pursue; ask for a research team member from each partner; and present the final plan.

If after you approach members and make a presentation (Chapters 3, 4, and 5) the

OPM ENTREPRENEUR RESOURCES

Focus groups are particularly favored by larger companies as an effective research tool. Two books that can help you discuss focus groups are *Focus Group Research Handbook*, by Holly Edmunds (McGraw-Hill, 2000), which is geared toward how to hire a market research company to conduct your research, and *Focus Groups: A Step-by-Step Guide* by Gloria E. Bader and Catherine A. Rossi (The Bader Group, 2002), which is geared toward conducting your own focus group research.

partners don't immediately agree, get a list of their concerns, in particular the research and facts that they'd like to see before proceeding. After noting their comments, ask if it would be all right to prepare a list of action items to address those concerns. Then come back and present to each partner the action items it mentioned, the ones your other partner mentioned, and other action items that you thought of, to see which items the partners think should be pursued. If you feel that your list is short, you can get help from SCORE or from your local Small Business Development Center (or other small business assistance centers in your area) to complete a respectable list of options. Make a thorough list, because your partners will use it to judge your competence. At the end of the list, state which options you think should be pursued. Show your list to the partners, ask if they have other options they'd like to consider, and then see if they agree with your recommended options. Once you agree on the options you will pursue, ask each partner for the name of a contact you can meet with or who can help you with the research. The partners' team members may play just a small role, but you will be helping the partners become more involved with the project, which will eventually help them decide to proceed with an introduction.

OBTAIN COMMITMENTS TO MOVE FORWARD

You need to know what level of positive results you must obtain to allow the project to go forward. The biggest mistake OPM entrepreneurs make is that they feel their partner companies will decide whether or not to proceed based on the same test results that will satisfy the entrepreneur. This is not likely to be the case, because the partners will have different criteria. The partners are not likely to give you a firm statement; they will probably tell you that they will just wait to see what the results are and then decide. You want a firmer commitment that that, and you can often get it by making a list of outcomes and asking which ones a partner would consider positive enough to move ahead; writing a letter to the other partner explaining the results that the first partner would need to move forward; and then meeting with the first partner to get his okay to send the letter.

For the next step, start with the list of actions that you and your partners have decided on. Then list what you feel would be extremely positive results. For example, at a trade show, you could have twenty or more retailers express strong interest in your idea, or a focus group could have two-thirds of the participants rate your service as their first choice. Then list other outcomes, all that are positive, but start at a level you would consider just barely passing, with maybe four levels of response between just passing and a strong result. For example, at a trade show, you could list that positive responses from three, five, ten, and fifteen retailers would be other options. You want to offer levels of results so that you can understand the point at which your partners feel that the test produces a passing grade.

Next, show the outcomes to your contact at the partner company and get feedback on which outcomes he or she feels will show the project has potential. With that information, compose a letter to the second partner, explaining what the first partner will consider a positive result. Then revisit your contact, explain that the other partner has requested some type of feedback about what kind of test results would be positive, and ask for the first partner's approval. This set of tactics might not work, as the contact at the one partner might not be willing to do or approve anything that could be viewed as a commitment, but generally the tactic will help you at least get some understanding of what the partner will consider passing results that justify moving ahead.

PROVIDE A TIMETABLE AND BUDGET

Next, create a timetable to list the steps that the partners want. Decide which ones to do first, and then estimate the costs of each step. You should have friendly contacts in partner companies who can help you estimate the costs of each step. If partners can't help, you can obtain costs from outside service firms, such as a prototype supplier, or a market research firm for items related to its activities. You can get costs for items like yours by attending trade shows and by calling up vendors to get quotes. Don't include the person responsible on the timetable just yet; you should do that only after you have approval from the partners to move ahead. I've included a sample timetable and budget for the project described earlier in the chapter—operational financing for companies with high levels of overseas outsourcing.

PROJECT DEVELOPMENT SCHEDULE:
FINANCING FOR OVERSEAS PRODUCTION

Activity	Costs	Time to Complete
Prepare sample sales collateral	$300	2 weeks
Call on three large prospects	$300	1 week
Call on three mid-size prospects	$300	1 week
Call on three small prospects	$300	1 week
Determine prospects' current finance charges	$0	1 week
Explore whether prospects would increase imports with financing	$200	2 weeks
Obtain financial data from interested prospects	$0	1 week
Determine costs for setting up warehouse space	$0	3 weeks
Determine whether prospects' finances justify financing	$100	2 weeks
Determine costs of setting up financing group	$1,500	3 weeks

CONVINCING PARTNERS TO PAY

You want partners to contribute to the project development phase, because paying for part of the project helps them become more committed to the project. In the example of the overseas production financing project, each partner will probably be happy to pick up its share of the costs to further investigate the project. Not all projects will have low costs like the one in the example, and in those cases you might need to convince partners to pick up the costs. You can typically get monetary support for the project if you pick up some of the costs yourself and then ask the marketing and provider partners to pick up the costs related to their activities.

There will always be inexpensive tasks that you can pay for on your own, or there will be certain tasks that take time and effort but don't cost any money. These are ideal for the OPM entrepreneurs to take on first. Make sure that they are tasks you know how to do, or can get help doing. The worst thing you can do is to take on a task and do a poor job in this development phase, because you could destroy the partners' confidence in you.

The next step is to approach the marketing partner whose tasks typically revolve around market research. These tasks might cost the partner money, but more than likely the partner will be able to accomplish the tasks with current staff and minimal additional expense over and above what it is already spending. The marketing partner is also the key to a project's going ahead, and once you have the marketing partner signed on to pay for its market research costs, you will be in the best position to entice an investment from the potential provider partner. You should be able to convince the marketing partner to agree to most if not all of the marketing-oriented tasks on your lists, because those costs will be modest.

Once you have the marketing partner on board, you can approach the provider partner. In the example of the outsource financing OPM deal, the provider's costs were low (simply investigating the legal steps and costs to set up a new finance group), and in fact not much more than the marketing group's costs; in this case, the provider would probably move ahead. But many times the costs left to the provider are much higher than those for the marketing company. The provider's decision-makers have two conflicting issues running through their minds. One is that they don't like to invest substantially more than the other partners do; at the same time, the provider doesn't want to lose this deal, especially if the marketing partner is well established and has a strong reputation. The provider knows that you may be able to find another provider if it doesn't want to pick up the provider-related costs in the project. It will probably pick up most of the costs if it has the money, but it might not. If the provider is reluctant, ask, "Is this a deal stopper for you? I'm not sure what the marketing partner will do, but I am willing to talk to them if it is. What worries me is that the marketing partner can respond with any of three choices: pick up part of the costs, ask me to look for another provider, or drop out of the deal. Since two of the three choices are bad, I'd rather not approach the marketer to pay for some of the production costs." If the provider still won't spend on

Market Reality

OPM partners will evaluate your deal versus other projects that they have available. Part of your selection process was finding partners that don't have many choices for new introductions, since those are the partners who will be eager to move ahead with you. If partners are reluctant to pay modest costs, they may be considering some of their alternatives, or they may just not be that excited about your concept. Ask the potential partners what concepts they will introduce if they don't move forward with yours. A partner may have found its own idea to pursue; in that case, you would be better off pursuing another partner.

prototypes or other production-related items, you will need to talk to the marketing partner.

The marketing partner will probably not be happy at first about paying for part of the provider's research and development costs. The partner will almost always assume that the provider is short of money, a perception that will make the marketing partner nervous about the project's success. The marketer will generally respond favorably if you explain that the provider is paying substantially more than is the marketing partner, and that it just wants to see a stronger commitment from the marketing partner by having it invest in part of the development expenses. Sometimes the marketer will give money, sometimes not. If your costs are uncovered and the marketer won't help, go back and tell the provider that it looks like the deal is at an impasse and that it might not be able to go through unless there is a change in the companies involved. Tell the provider you will just have to think about what to do. Then wait a few weeks to see if either the provider or marketer changes its mind. If neither one does, you will have to decide which partner is more important and then try to replace the partner that you think is less crucial.

CORRECTIVE ACTIONS

Most development projects have several surprising twists, whether it is in building models or service concepts or in conducting market research, and you and your partners will have to deal with them. The main reason I recommended that you ask for each partner to designate someone to your development project is so you can talk about the results of the research and ask for the contacts' help in interpreting the results. Your contacts won't be surprised that things didn't quite go as expected, and they should be able to help you decide what to report to the management.

Don't assume immediately that some negative feedback will stop your deal, or even pose a problem. You may not be accustomed to seeing typical results from market testing, which frequently are both positive and negative. Often, the end-user and distribution channel results that you think are negative won't bother the partner at all. If your contacts believe that a little more testing is needed, just go back and initiate a new budget and timeline. If you follow the advice in the next chapter, which deals with setting up your deal to encourage quick action on the partners' part, you might be able to skip any further research and development unless your results are extremely bad.

SEVEN

KEEP THE DEAL IN YOUR POCKET: FIND THE KEY INGREDIENT FOR CONTROL

There is a danger that the OPM entrepreneur can easily be eased out of the new venture he or she has proposed. This could happen even if the entrepreneur has a patent, trademark, or other intellectual property rights. Fortunately you have many options for gaining control in an OPM deal. You can use some of your own money to hire a manufacturer or to help pay for tooling. You can buy from the manufacturer and resell to the marketer. You have contractual agreements that protect your position, forcing partners to have your approval before changes are made. One unmistakable fact, though, is that you had better have control in the original agreements or you will never regain it. The best way for you to have control is to add real value to the venture so that partners will want your continued involvement.

The last chapter discussed the importance of signing a Letter of Intent and Mutual Confidentiality Agreement before disclosing too many details about your deal. The LOI also spells out that there will potentially be an agreement signed that will impact all three parties. Keep in mind, though, that counting on legal documents can be dangerous. If things go wrong, your only remedy is to sue the partners, thereby guaranteeing an end to the project's chance of success.

Bringing a valued asset to the partners is a tactic you need to strive for, even if what you can offer is not immediately obvious to you.

In Chapter 3, we discussed how to look professional in packaging your concept, and Chapter 6 offered tactics that help you control the process in the research phase so that you'll be respected by your partners. The goal of this chapter is to address how to actually collect the money you've earned and deserve for setting up the OPM deal. You'll learn how you can structure a deal to have control; this might include investing in it yourself, or utilizing intellectual property protection such as trademarks and patents. It certainly involves putting the right clauses in contract agreements and, most important, determining a valuable role you can play that contributes to the project's success. In the end, you will have the best results if you are involved in the production and sale of the concept from the day the project starts until the day it ends. This chapter will:

- Explain when you might want to invest, and how you, or partners, can invest at the last moment
- Discuss the role that patents and other intellectual property protection can play
- Describe deal structures that OPM entrepreneurs can use to keep control
- Offer the types of roles entrepreneurs might play to enhance their value
- List agreement negotiating points you need to consider in all of your conversations about a deal structure

MAXIMIZING CONTROL

Stan Everette created Perfect-Caulk, an easy-to-use caulking gun that lays down a perfect bead every time. Everette first obtained his patent before doing anything else, and he then decided that he couldn't get anywhere without a prototype. Since the cost was only a few thousand dollars, he paid for it on his own. Everette's next step after having the prototype created was to check out how he wanted to have the product marketed. He didn't want to have his own sales force and he didn't want to use a master distributor, which would require too many discounts in the distribution channel. (Master distributors sell to other distributors, who then sell to retailers.) Everette approached three people to be the marketer—a large Canadian retail chain (he lives in Canada) and two distributors. All committed to carrying the product on normal terms (the same discount structure at which they would buy from an established manufacturer) for two years with nonexclusive agreements. Everette had done a good job so far: he was able to secure his marketing partners without any loss of control.

Everette was worried about manufacturers stealing his idea; his product could easily be made by manufacturers with the proper equipment, and he wasn't sure his patent could prevent competitors from developing a slightly different product. So he approached three potential provider companies, and found that all were willing to produce Perfect-Caulk and to put up tooling costs and offer extended terms. Everette decided not to use the manufacturers' money, and instead paid for the tooling himself. He then split up the manufacturing duties, having one company make the injected molded parts and another company assemble the unit. The companies also continued to offer Everette extended terms so that his operational cash flow was minimal.

Everette works from his kitchen table, without employees, and takes orders, arranges shipments (to just a handful of distributors and retailers), and bills after shipment. The manufacturers make the product and offer extended terms, and the marketers pay for the deliveries within thirty to forty days. Everette's total investment—for patent, prototype, and an initial production run—was $14,000. Today his product is selling more than $1.5 million annually, and his wise investment gave Everette total control over his product line. Everette could have gone the OPM route of not putting up any money (except for the patent) at several points, but the higher profits of investing versus his modest investment costs made his deal very sweet. In the final analysis, most of the money invested in the project still belongs to the manufacturers, who covered the operating costs of producing Perfect-Caulk, including owning the raw material inventory. Everette still does very little of the actual work that makes his product a success. He has found a way to obtain the OPM benefit of low start-up costs, while still receiving all of the profits, a benefit usually reserved for traditional entrepreneurs.

INVESTING YOURSELF OR GETTING INVESTORS

In many ways the OPM process is a door opener. You might start out with a promising concept but without any money, so you might not be able to introduce your concept without partners. In that case, you have to settle for whatever control you can obtain. But as you walk through the OPM process, your situation changes. When the project is ready to go, all of a sudden you have a marketing partner who likes the idea and is willing to support it, and a provider willing to both produce and invest in the idea. At this point you have a concept that is much less risky and much more interesting as an investment. If you have friends or acquaintances with money, or are able to invest money yourself, you might be in a position in which an investment looks like an attractive option. You might be burdened by some of the commitments you've made in your LOIs, but your partners will probably accommodate your desire to invest if you approach them carefully. To maximize your participation in your concept's profits you should understand investing advantages; know how to calculate the return on an OPM investment; and understand how to approach the partners to escape any commitments they may have agreed to under an LOI.

Investment Benefits

The two benefits of investing are control and a bigger share of the profits. You typically have more say in the project if you invest, and with an investment you can more easily negotiate a deal in which you exert independent control, as you would, for example, if you bought from the provider and sold to the marketer. Without an investment, an OPM entrepreneur might have to settle for receiving a commission or other type of percentage of sales payment, which might imply that the OPM entrepreneur provides a service rather than has ownership in the project.

OPM deals also split profits three ways. If you can turn a partner from an investor to a provider, as Stan Everette did with his manufacturing partners, that party will have less control and will only receive profits that are standard for a contract manufacturer. That leaves more income for the OPM entrepreneur. In some cases you might not be able to invest enough to take out a partner's ownership position, but you still may be able to increase your share of the profits with an investment. For example, a provider might, if you pick up some of the costs, drop its extra charge for assuming start-up and operating costs from a 3 percent premium to a 1.5 percent premium.

Calculating Your Return

You don't want to invest unless it is a good deal for you, so calculate the return on your investment before putting up any money. You will receive some share of the profits even if you don't have an investment. Calculate your investment return based only on the difference between the money you will receive without an investment and the money you will receive with an investment.

Consider the example of Perfect-Caulk. The product was sold to distributors for approximately $2.00. That price would be the same with or without Everette's investment. But the manufacturer's price to Everette might have been $1.50 without an investment, and $1.45 if Everette paid for the tooling. On shipments of one million units, that five cents per unit adds up to $50,000 per year. That's a great return on an investment of $14,000.

What could you do if $50,000 was needed for investment and you didn't have that much money? Just let the manufacturer pick up the costs? Maybe, but you could also consider looking for an investment from people you know, or an independent investor. A $50,000 annual return on a $50,000 investment is a 100 percent return, which is pretty darn good. Even if you split the $50,000 annual profit with the investor, the investor would still make $25,000 per year for a $50,000 investment, which is a 50 percent return.

Escaping Commitments

You also may need to know how to escape any earlier promises you may have made that offered to take a low share of the profits in return for not making an investment. Your problem as an OPM entrepreneur is that the investment will not look safe or attractive until the project really falls together with the marketer and provider on board. To keep things moving up to that time and to protect your position in the deal, you might sign an LOI or other agreement that outlines how the parties will interact, including how the parties will handle the investment of the project. The LOI probably stated that you will have little or no investment, and it might have impacted tentative statements about the profit-sharing arrangements of the project.

OPM entrepreneurs have two things going for them that will allow them to typically escape their commitments. One is that the LOI is just a guideline, and it clearly states that you will be negotiating a final contract. That means you can negotiate a different deal if you dramatically change the partners' mix of investments (including your investment). Second, both partners would rather see you invest more than you originally promised. That larger investment shows that you have confidence in the idea; more important, it means that you have something to lose if things don't go well. That gives the partners more confidence that you'll do your part in making the project a success.

PATENTS AND TRADEMARKS

Patents offer some degree of a competitive advantage, and owning a patent can open doors for an OPM entrepreneur. Trademarks are also assets if you have a great name for the product or service, or a strong phrase describing its benefits, but they aren't nearly as powerful as many OPM entrepreneurs think they are. Don't let down your guard; always protect yourself through confidentiality agreements, LOIs, and other agreements that have strong protection for you.

If your concept is a product, patents do have value, primarily because your partners expect you to have them. Having a patent helps establish that you are committed to your idea. But you don't need a patent; you can instead state that you are waiting to finalize your design before you obtain a patent but in the meantime are taking several steps to protect your patent rights. The steps you can mention are keeping an inventor's notebook, which will cost about $30 (go to *www.cleansweepsupply.com* or *www.eurekalabbook.com*), and registering your product with the Patent Office's Document Disclosure Program, at a cost of $10 (*www.uspto.gov/web/offices/pac/disdo.html*). For $25 you can obtain a copy of the document back from the patent office. The Document Disclosure Program doesn't offer you any real protection, but it registers your idea and documents a date on which you can prove that you created the idea. Because America has "invented first" patent laws (which state that whoever comes up with an idea first has the right to patent it, even if someone else applies for the patent first), documenting the date of your product creation protects your ability to patent the concept.

The reason you don't want to overly rely on a patent is that patents are for a very specific product design, and not for a broad category of products. As an example, Mr. Coffee, the first electric drip coffeemaker, came out with several patents, but in no time at all Mr. Coffee had several competitors, all with their own patents. The patent didn't protect the concept of an electric drip coffeemaker; it only protected Mr. Coffee's specific design. Chances are pretty good that your partners may be able to figure out another way to make your idea if they really want to. You minimize the chances of the partners' doing that by signing a Mutual Confidentiality Agreement and LOI no matter what your patent status is.

FINDING A ROLE

John Lawler worked for an airline and felt that both the typical video screens in the front of planes and the newer embedded systems with screens in the back of each seat had many drawbacks. First, everyone had to watch the same movie at the same time, and in the case of the big video screens, some people couldn't see the movie well. Also, if the movie system went out, no one could watch the movie. To top it off, the entire system was expensive. A big problem of the embedded systems with screens on each seat was that they were too expensive, costing between $500,000 and $1,000,000 to install per plane.

Lawler thought that a much better idea was just having individual movie players that could attach to the back of a seat. Players would only cost $200 to $400 each, or less than $100,000 for a typical plane. The individual units could operate without the cabin crew's assistance, and they could be leased to the plane. Passengers could then select the movies they wanted, and select when they wanted to start, pause, or stop a movie. The problem for Lawler was that the movie players were already invented; his idea was just to have the maker of the movie player lease them to airlines. What role and what value could he add to his project?

Lawler's solution was to create a role that licensed the movies and reprogrammed the players monthly. He took the initiative to work a deal to license movies with a major movie studio, and then he made a deal with the movie studios for a license fee that allowed him to reprogram the players every month at a nominal fee. To sweeten his deal, Lawler leased the movie players from the manufacturer, which was willing to front the equipment to Lawler because he had a lease from the airline. Lawler then offered a licensing fee, which included both the player manufacturer's fee and an additional fee for licensing the movies and reprogramming the players.

A DEAL STRUCTURE TO KEEP CONTROL

As a rule, you can execute the most control in deals in which you take title to the invoice, such as buying from the provider and selling to the marketer. You have even more control in a deal like John Lawler's, in which the OPM entrepreneur doesn't just take ownership, but also adds value. The worst deal is one in which you receive a commission from the providers and you don't add any value. The following list explains a variety of deal structures you might use, starting from ones in which you have the most control to ones in which you have the least.

1. *Buy and sell, plus add value to the product or service.* In the airplane movie players example, the OPM entrepreneur buys, sells, and adds value. The licensing arrangements and the monthly reprogramming were the value added to the entrepreneur's service.

2. *Buy and sell and take possession.* You might inventory the product and ship it to smaller customers.

3. *Buy and sell, plus add non-product-related value to the project.* You could offer value by giving seminars, or by being on key committees at associations.

4. *Buy, sell, and hold intellectual property rights.* Both patents and trademarks offer you some additional leverage.

5. *Buy and sell.* This can be a paperwork transaction only, and you can delay payment until you get paid, but your position isn't strong if you don't also add value.

6. *Broker agreement.* This structure comes into play when you have several potential marketers and providers to work with. You have strong control unless some of the marketers or providers decide to go into the market on their own.

7. *Full partnership or a three-way contract agreement.* You are a full partner, but only have 33 percent control and can consistently be outvoted unless the contract states that all partners need to agree to major decisions.

8. *Receive a percentage from the provider, hold intellectual property rights, and provide value.* This could be adding value by selling the product, by being connected to end users or the market, or by providing engineering and product development.

9. *Receive percentage from the provider and hold intellectual property rights.*

10. *Receive commission from marketer and provide value by being connected to the end user, or by offering value to the marketer's sales effort.*

11. *Cost-sharing proposals.* If the marketer picks up some of the provider's costs, the marketer will sooner or later end up with almost total control of the project. Try to avoid cost sharing of provider expenses unless you are providing the extra investment.

12. *A percentage from the provider, with you providing limited value.*

13. *A percentage from the marketer, with you providing limited value.*

ROLES TO PLAY

The OPM entrepreneur has a very strong interest in finding a role she can play that will keep her as an important team member, both to maintain some control and to maximize her profits. The roles you can play fall into four categories: being connected to the end user's world (an infiltration marketer); independently performing a part of the product or service production; adding value to the sales efforts; and providing assistance to the provider. Because OPM deals vary tremendously, it is impossible to list every possible role, but the sections that follow

MARKET REALITY

If you must accept a percentage of sales, or commission, you want that percentage paid by the provider. You have less control, and a greater risk of being squeezed out, if you are receiving a percentage from the marketer. This is especially true if your value to the partners is in your market connections. Providers generally feel that they aren't good at marketing and are happy to listen to your input and to allow you to collect your percentage for the life of the contract without complaining. Marketers, on the other hand, want to be connected to end users, and they will want to know all your market connections. Once they know what you do, they probably won't be interested in your input, or even worse, they'll question why they should be paying you.

should help you think creatively to find a role that suits your talents and gives you strong control.

Connection to the End Users' World

These roles, which I call *infiltration marketing* because you become a part of the customers' world, are highly valued by your partners; they offer you more control and, better yet, the insights that could expand the project with more peripheral and derivative products. End users' needs and desires dictate most business decisions and generate most new market concepts. Some of the ways you can be connected to the end users' world are:

- Being an end user, or ideally a key market influencer
- Knowing and meeting frequently with key market influencers
- Volunteering on association committees
- Offering seminars or training to end users
- Being associated with university or industry end-user studies or research
- Becoming a recognized expert in applications related to your concept

Independently Playing a Part in the Production Process

This applies to both product and service concepts. As an example, I mentioned earlier in the book a service that measures the loss of precious metal catalyst on a catalytic converter. The OPM entrepreneur could provide, as a key component of the service, a report comparing the theoretical catalyst loss to the actual loss and offer insights into why there was a difference. That report then would be shipped to the customer along with the actual test results. Other ways to play a role in the production process include:

- Assembling or packaging the product
- Inventorying the product and arranging shipment for small orders
- Selecting the best service provider for the contracts generated by the marketing partner
- Customizing products with instructions and packaging depending on the application
- Performing final quality inspection at the OPM entrepreneur's location
- Providing installation and operational training assistance
- Troubleshooting difficult service or installation problems

Marketing- and Sales-Related Activities

Partners will value any special sales or marketing assistance you can provide that will increase sales. Excellent connections to the key players in the market are appreciated, but you could also become a market specialist; for example, you could specialize in outsourcing companies' operational funding in order to assist the marketer's sales force in closing big deals. Valued roles you could play are:

- Product demonstrator at trade shows or for key customers
- Contact person who has relationships with one or more key customers
- Sales and service trainer for people in the distribution channel
- Technical specialist for sales at large accounts
- Street marketing or event marketing team organizer
- Ad assistant, helping to prepare marketing collateral material such as brochures, mailers, ads, or manuals
- Web site operator, running an interactive site and answering prospects' e-mailed questions

Providing Assistance to the Provider

Your product might be targeted at a new market for the provider, which has special requirements, or you might have expertise either in manufacturing or in providing service that could be useful to the provider. These services might also be useful to the marketer, but some OPM entrepreneurs aren't good at relating to end users or people in the distribution channel and are better off concentrating on helping the provider. Some roles that assist the provider are:

- Engineering assistance
- End-user interface, helping to determine product specifications
- New product development—you might have several ways to improve the first-generation product or service, with better costs, performance, or reliability
- Troubleshooting quality and performance problems
- Quality oversight for service work
- Managing the service network
- Training provider service personnel
- Customer service; conducting follow-up customer satisfaction surveys

OPM ENTREPRENEUR RESOURCES

Write Your Own Business Contract: What Your Attorney Won't Tell You by E. Thorpe Barrett (3rd Edition, Oasis Press, 2000) is a guide that is easy to understand even if you've never seen a contract before. I've used the first edition of this book for almost ten years, and I refer to it at least three to four times per year. The goal of the book isn't to bypass your attorney, but rather to allow you to structure a rough agreement so you can first understand what the agreement will eventually say and also cut down on your attorney costs. Also look into *www.agreementsetc.com*, a site that sells low-cost agreement forms that you can use as a starting point for your own agreements.

AGREEMENT CLAUSES TO CONSIDER EARLY ON

Chapter 10 covers agreements between partners, but certain elements of eventual OPM agreements dealing with control are important to understand during all of your conversations and need to be included in your LOI. You need to protect your turf from the start or you will have trouble protecting yourself in the final agreement. For example, if the marketer feels that you are acting as a representative of the provider, you are going to have trouble turning yourself into a full partner when the final contracts are struck. While you might not end up with everything you want, I can guarantee you'll end up with a whole lot less if you don't stake out key positions early. In some cases, OPM deals will be completed with just buy-and-sell agreements or other simple contracts, and you won't need to worry as much about control clauses. But if you feel that you may end up with a two-way or three-way agreement or partnership, make sure to frame the following six points into your early conversations with partners as well as your LOIs and final agreements.

1.   *You are a separate entity and partner.* Marketers in particular will try to make you a representative or agent of the provider, especially if you end up receiving a commission. You might not actually be partners in your agreements, but rather three separate entities; however, in spirit, you are partners all working to introduce your concept.

2.   *Your share of the profits is based on having created the idea as well as your role in the project.* If you accept that your compensation is based on your duties, then you run into several problems. One is that you will be treated as a minor partner if your duties are less than those of the other partners. A second is that one of the partners might want to take over your duties and cut you out of the deal.

3. *All partners will grant other partners the right of first refusal to participate in next-generation, derivative, and peripheral products.* You don't want partners to come up with a whole series of new products that are a result of your concept and leave you out. Participation in the new products or services could be either an extension of the current agreement to cover the new products, or a new agreement.

4. *Agreements are for a minimum of three years.* Five years is even better, but that is hard to execute. Three years is enough time for partners to recover their investments and for you to make a tidy profit.

5. *Non-disclosure agreement clauses will survive the termination of the contract.* You don't want any of the partners to keep producing your concept after the agreement has ended and exclude your participation. If the project continues to sell, you should participate.

6. *All partners must mutually agree to changes in the concept's features, configuration, and pricing, or a major change in how any of the partners approaches its roles and responsibilities.* You want to avoid having one partner make changes that allow it to reap a higher percentage of the profits or make changes that could impact the concept's marketability. You can check your partners' ability to do either by having changes approved by all the partners.

EIGHT

DELIVER A QUICK START-UP: OFFER AN EASY DECISION TO YOUR PARTNERS

OPM entrepreneurs usually are wheeler-dealers, free spirits ready to take a chance. Partner companies, on the other hand, will almost always be more cautious, and sometimes much more cautious. OPM entrepreneurs are ready to go right into a full sales mode, but companies are slow to align their resources behind a new concept, primarily because they probably have had dozens of new product or service failures in their history. For every marketing person at a company chomping at the bit to get started, there will be others who are trying to rein the project in. The tests you did with the partner companies (covered in Chapter 6) have more or less established that the product has appeal and that it could be made at a price that would produce profits. Once testing is finished and you complete a financial analysis with the partners' help, you are ready to kick off the project and start the business rolling.

A request for a market test, which is a standard procedure at most companies, often comes next. This will almost always rub an OPM entrepreneur the wrong way: "Oh no, not another delay. Will we ever get started?" I take the opposite view; this is the best news you could have. A market test offers you the opportunity to have a quick sales start in a small market and get the project going with a big head of steam. You can run the first test with just a few people in the company, with temporary tooling, or other very low start-up costs, and get the project on the market right away. You have a much better chance to sign a full-scale deal once a company starts selling, even in a small way. The request for a market test allows you and the partners to start quickly, with low costs, and provides an easy entry point for partners. They typically can make the decision for a market test quickly, versus a long and slow decision on a full-scale introduction. Another advantage of a market test is that you can have a major influence on the test's being successful, while you'll not be able to exert nearly as much influence in a full market launch.

Think of the market test as a quick start where partners will let you play a major role, because you can expedite the test. It is also a sales test in which you can use a variety of tactics that will raise your probability for success. What could possibly be better? In this chapter, the goal is to get you through the defining moment of the OPM deal process: getting partners past the "I'm interested but nervous" phase to the point at which they will offer a commitment to move ahead. You have several tasks to perform in launching the project's test: leveraging partners against each other to keep momentum; finding a low-cost, easy-to-execute market test; and participating in the test in a manner that will improve your odds for success. This chapter will:

- Cover how to play the marketing and provider partners off each other
- List options for finding a source of supply for the test
- Explain how to find a test market with a strong chance of success
- Discuss options to help the first test program succeed
- Show how you need to take the lead in getting the project done
- Explain how to limit a test program's scope to keep costs modest

- Cover how to get partners to buy into specific goals
- Discuss why it's advantageous for sales to go through you and why that is sometimes better for the partners
- Offer timelines to ensure that the project gets moving as quickly as possible

UNANSWERED QUESTIONS SEAL THE DEAL

Patricia Manion, a biology and chemistry major, was working her way through school as a hairdresser. She specialized in long braids, primarily for African-American women. Many of her customers had their own hair braided but then also used extensions, which were glued into their hair, to produce the exact look they were looking for. Every so often, about once per month, they needed to come back to get the glue out, either to change the hairstyle or to clean their hair. Getting the glue out was tough to do at all and even tougher to do well. Manion thought what the market needed was a formula to quickly and completely clean out the glue.

Manion worked on her concept at school and, with the help of some of her professors, she was able to develop a cleaning formula that would take down the hair extensions and thoroughly clean out the glue in less than ten minutes. Manion tried the product at her own salon for a few months to work out the bugs, and, once some of her colleagues successfully used her product on some of their own customers, she was ready to go.

Patricia talked to the salesperson of a distributor that called on the salon where she worked and asked her what she thought should be her next step. The salesperson set up a meeting for Manion with the president of the company, which, as it turned out, distributed products in twenty-four states. The distributor stated that he would partner with Manion and market the product, provided he received positive feedback from fifteen market-influencing stylists and the product could be sold for less than $8 for an eight-ounce bottle.

Step one went well, as twelve of the fifteen stylists thought the product was far better than anything they had used before to get out glue, but the $8 price for an eight-ounce bottle was another issue. Manion had found a small chemical company that could make her product. But to hit a cost of $4 (a 50 percent margin on an $8 purchase) the manufacturer needed to invest in some new equipment and needed to produce 50,000 bottles per year. The distributor wouldn't guarantee that level of sales because it wasn't sure how many bottles a typical salon might buy. The deal looked like it might be in jeopardy.

Manion felt strongly that the market was much bigger than 50,000 bottles a year. She convinced her partners to run a market test in her hometown of Atlanta. The manufacturer could make small quantities of the product for $7 per bottle, not low enough to produce profits, but still good enough so the test wouldn't lose money. The distributor committed two salespeople to sell the product in Atlanta. Once the test started, Manion spent twenty to thirty hours per week calling on salons, selling her product to support the two sales representatives. After six months, first-time sales and then reorder sales indicated that the distributor could sell as many as 200,000 bottles per year. With that volume, the distributor and manufacturer committed and the deal went forward.

LEVERAGING THE PARTNERS

On most projects you may occasionally need to leverage the partners off of each other to keep the ball rolling. The basic problem that OPM entrepreneurs face is that their potential partners have plenty of projects to work on, and they can easily let their work on the OPM deal slip for several months. You can't let that happen, because one or both of your partners could possibly withdraw if the deal loses its momentum. This risk is especially strong in the market test, because the OPM concept's test sales will have a minimal impact on the company's quarterly results.

To keep the project moving, you may need to push both partners to do their part to launch the tests. Ideally, all partners will jump right in and work full speed on the project. If they don't, you will need to accelerate everyone's efforts. If you need to speed up the marketing, tell your contacts that the provider isn't sure that the marketer is moving full speed ahead, and that the provider is considering scaling back its efforts to get products ready for sale. If the provider is moving slowly, tell your contact that the marketer is ready to roll and is wondering what is taking the provider so long to get products ready. If the partners are still moving slowly, remind them what a big market opportunity is in front of all of you and that one partner's lagging behind could easily kill the deal.

FINDING SUPPLY

The key to getting a market test underway quickly is to find supply that has low overall costs and that you can obtain fairly quickly. You don't need a low production cost for the test; in fact, no one will be overly upset if you sell the product for a loss. However, low total costs—which include tooling, marketing materials, and the cost of a minimum order quantity—count heavily. Low costs encourage people to move ahead with the test. This isn't necessarily easier for a service than it is for a product, because your service might call for extensive programming, expensive equipment, and in-depth training of personnel. In some cases it costs almost as much to prepare a service for a test as it is to prepare for a full introduction. Don't worry if there are modest or reasonable costs; you should be able to get your partners to pick them up, as you learned to do for research costs in Chapter 6. The steps listed below are ones that should get you started in your search to obtain low total costs, but don't be afraid to look at other sources if you see another way to get the low costs you need. Hopefully one of the first of the following steps will work and you'll be on your way, but if not, keep going down the list to find a solution that works.

1. *Ask what your provider partner can do.* Your provider partner might be able to make the supply you need with temporary tooling, by assigning two service representatives to your project, or by modifying some existing parts to work on your product concept.

2. *Ask provider contacts for advice.* They have undoubtedly faced this challenge before and might have some suggestions about other providers you can use, or other ways to have a small supply of product available.

3. *Get a cost and test the waters.* The cost you have now may look high to you, but don't prejudge your partners. Your partners might think the deal is just fine if the total cost is $12,000 to get 3,000 units to sell at $2.99. Before continuing to the next steps, check to be sure the partners believe that the cost you have now is too high before you assume that it is.

4. *Divide the product or service into components.* Often you can get components, both for service and products, from various suppliers and assemble them into a product or service combination that will demonstrate that the project will work.

5. *Find suppliers for components.* Try to find smaller companies that are accustomed to production that requires step-by-step processing rather than expensive tooling. Your provider contacts can help you find these suppliers if you are having trouble.

6. *Bring your costs to your partners again.* They may feel that the price from this step is acceptable, or they might even decide the

costs you had earlier, which were for a true representation of the final concept, provide a better value.

7. *Look at components and check for shortcuts.* Pick out the components with the highest costs relative to their value and try to determine another, lower-cost method to supply that component. You might want to check with a SCORE advisor (*www.score.org*) if you are having trouble coming up with an innovative solution.

8. *Ask partners for suggestions.* Your contacts at companies have experience troubleshooting problems and they might have suggestions about other steps you can take to generate supply. If they understand that you can't cut the costs any more, they might also be willing to accept some of the earlier prices that they felt were too high.

A TEST PROVES THE CONCEPT HAS VALUE

Zairil Khalid suffered from diabetes and learned early that keeping his blood sugar levels right was a difficult task. The challenge was that insulin dosages were set based on the average of all diabetics, while in fact each patient is affected in different ways by different types of food and exercise. Khalid wasn't willing to rely only on his doctor's use of an average insulin response to food or exercise; he wanted to know exactly what his responses were, and he felt that other diabetic patients would also want more control of their disease.

Khalid's concept was to start a service that would allow diabetics to send in a two-day diary of the food they ate and their exercise activity either five or twenty times per month, so that patients could start to see the impact of specific foods and exercises. That would allow each patient to design his or her own regimen, which would call for using as little insulin as possible.

Khalid was able to interest two Web sites and one association, all dedicated to and run by diabetics, in marketing the service. To provide the service, he found a medical laboratory that could take blood sugar readings from diabetics and then run the readings through a computer program that would determine the impact of food and the exercise content of daily activities for each client.

The marketing partners had seen preliminary tests that looked impressive, but they were concerned that testing a large sample of people would not show enough patient-to-patient difference to make the service worthwhile; they felt that patients' readings might not differ that much from the averages that doctors used. The marketing partners wanted the system tried out on 100 people for four months to see how much variance really existed from one patient to the next.

Khalid's problem was that the computer program that would correlate blood sugar to a diary was a difficult and expensive program to produce, and the laboratory wasn't willing to make the investment for a test of 100 patients when the test results might kill the project. Khalid was able to run the test by recruiting 15 volunteers from the diabetic groups associated with his marketing partners to manually review the data and determine the impact of foods and exercise. The process of manually going through the decision matrix for each patient was time consuming but worthwhile in the end, because the patient-to-patient differences from both food and exercise were significant.

CHOOSE THE TEST MARKET

The ideal market has easy access to end users, is covered by a strong, supportive sales representative of the marketing company, has a large group of end users that need your product, and is somewhat close to your home. You want to be scouting for a good test market while you are trying to locate supply for the test so that you can immediately suggest the test market to attack once supply is identified.

Easy access to end users and a strong, supportive sales representative are the two most important keys to selecting a market. For example, if you have a bike product, you could face three market situations: markets dominated by national companies; markets dominated by local or regional chains; and markets dominated by smaller bike dealers. The easiest access to the market is through larger local chains; local chains are much easier to sell to than are national chains and are more convenient to sell to than a large number of small stores would be. The same situation can exist in service businesses. In the example of the diabetes monitoring service, a market with strong diabetes support groups, or a large clinic specializing in diabetes, offers much easier access than does a market without a support group or specialized clinics.

In most marketing organizations, 10 to 30 percent of the salespeople are top performers. You want a market test in an area where the salesperson has many strong contacts and can get buyers to try out your product. You can often find the top salespeople by telling the marketing partner that you would like to interview a few of the company's top salespeople to get their feedback on the features, benefits, and price of your concept. In many cases, though not always, you will get the names of top salespeople. Your conversations with those salespeople should let you know which one is most supportive of your concept. You also want a test market in an area where the salesperson or personnel are very excited about your idea.

Certain markets have many more targeted customers than do others, and you'll have the best tests if you enter a market where there are many potential customers. The last consideration is to have the market somewhat close to your home. That's important because you want to help the test period to be a big success, and you can make that happen by aggressively promoting your concept in the market. You simply can do more promotion if you live close to where the test is occurring.

CREATING SUCCESS

One of the nice features of a test program is that you can go out and impact a large part of the market by running programs, including hosting special events and seminars, offering co-op advertising programs, doing demonstrations on weekends, and helping the marketer's sales representative sell your service. The range of special work you can do changes depending on your concept, but you should initiate at least three or four programs in the test market. A variety of options are listed below to get you started in your creative thinking for promoting your concept. Your promotions may not produce enough sales to cover their costs, but that is not important; what counts is that you have a successful test period.

1. Special events: For service concepts you can bring in an industry-known speaker and host a luncheon or afternoon event discussing how participants can profit from new trends and developments in the market. You can also host booths at consumer events that are related to your concept.

2. In-store demonstrations and sampling on weekends.

OPM ENTREPRENEUR RESOURCES

If you haven't had much experience in marketing a product or service, a great reference is *Getting Business to Come to You* by Paul and Sarah Edwards and Laura Clampitt Douglas (2nd Edition, Tarcher/Putnam, 1998). This book is targeted at home-based business and focuses on low-cost, relatively easy-to-execute strategies. The third section is right on target for test-marketing tactics, focusing on low-cost tactics including clever mailings, press release programs, and cross-promotions.

3. Special promotions such as co-op advertising, promotional giveaways, and contests.

4. Training of salespeople in the distribution channel, including working in the stores or traveling with salespeople.

5. Your own network of contacts to help jump-start sales (another reason to run the test program close to home).

6. Free installation and end-user training at the customer site.

7. Additional services or features or extra components at no charge for initial customers.

8. Special mailings to targeted customers offering incentives for a quick purchase.

9. Promotions that benefit groups or associations related to your target customer.

10. Press releases distributed to the local media.

TAKING CHARGE

Companies typically don't put out a new concept and just have it sit on a retailer's shelf, or put it in a salesperson's portfolio and hope it sells. But they sometimes will do that in a test market, because they are typically not accustomed to promoting a product on a small scale. For most introductions, a company appoints a marketing person or project manager who shepherds the product to the market and worries about how the product will sell in the test market. In an OPM deal that person is you. Though it may never be officially assigned to you, the responsibility for sourcing and promoting the concept for the test market will fall to you by default. That doesn't mean that you have to pay for the test program; partners can still be approached to help with the payment. But you will probably have to take charge by taking the lead on finding supply, creating a low-cost promotional program, creating a timeline and action plan, and managing the actual test market program.

While you may be in the lead, you still want to have contacts from your partner companies helping you. They have experience and can help you make better decisions, plus their participation keeps the partner involved in the project to keep their enthusiasm high, and they can also help you raise money from their company to pay for the project. You should explore your options for supply, put together some initial promotion concepts, prepare a preliminary action plan (see the upcoming section on timelines), and then present that plan to the partners. Explain that your plan is just a draft and then ask if your partner can designate a contact to help you during the test.

You might also approach the partners and ask a contact before doing any preliminary work. However, I don't recommend that tack, for two reasons. First, you want to establish your value to the partners, and the test market program is an area where you can contribute heavily, making a big difference in the test program's results. You'll probably not be able to make such a big impact ever again in the project. Second, you want to control the test market, and doing preliminary work will keep you in charge. Your contacts from your partners will have many other duties besides working on the test project, and so, while they will help, they will not be nearly as dedicated to your concept as you are.

LIMITING THE SCOPE

Modest costs are the result of low-cost supply and low-cost promotional tactics; another tactic to hold down costs is to limit the project's scope. You need your test market program to show partners that your concept will sell and meet market needs. But often you can do that with a test market program that is limited in scope just as well as you can with a much broader program. A project with limited scope will cut your supply, marketing, and promotion costs, and it will allow your individual efforts to produce the best benefit. For example, if you have a bike concept, a test market at a chain of ten bike stores is easy and inexpensive to execute, and proves just as well that a concept will sell as would a test that approaches every bike shop in New Jersey. The same rule applies in service projects. A test of the diabetic monitoring system conducted with patients at one or two clinics would be just as effective as trying to sell to diabetics throughout a major metropolitan area.

CLARIFY GOALS FOR SUCCESS

A test program is only worthwhile if you know when it is successful. You want to define that success before the test program starts. Otherwise you might find that partners are disappointed in what you feel are fabulously successful results. You have to take the lead in setting up a realistic goal for the test program. If you have a bike concept being tested in a chain of ten stores, what would a good result be? The best way to determine that is to choose six or seven products that are priced similarly and carried in the bike shop. Then determine about how many of each of those products would sell in three months. You might find this out from the store personnel or industry salespeople. Then compare the lists with your partners and decide, based on the sales of the other products, what everyone would consider an acceptable result from your test.

Service concept tests sometimes focus on customer benefits from the service rather than sales results. That's the case for the diabetic service discussed earlier; the question was how much difference really exists between an individual patient's reaction and the average patient's reaction to the same food and exercise. You and the partners might decide that the test is successful if patients' reactions to most items varied more than 30 percent from the average response, or, if the partners are more scientific-minded, if the standard deviation is over 15 percent of the median result.

WHO'S MAKING THE SALE?

Before you start the test and the timetable, there is one seemingly small item that you can use to your advantage: billing customers. Typically, the agreement paperwork is not all signed until the test period is over. Your most advantageous deal is when you buy and sell products under separate agreements with each party (see Chapter 6). But in a test period, there are costs picked up by the provider, costs picked up by the marketer, and cost picked by the OPM entrepreneur. Sometimes companies have trouble setting up their accounting systems to handle a new transaction that has three partners and costs that are split several ways.

You can offer to resolve that situation by doing the billing yourself and then splitting the revenue. Each partner can bill its out-of-pocket costs for the test to its normal accounts, and then just collect a percentage of the revenue, which they can record as income. A split might have the marketer with 15 to 20 percent of the revenue, the pro-

OPM ENTREPRENEUR RESOURCES

You are likely to end up on many teams with partners working to get your project rolling as quickly as possible. You can learn how to effectively function on these teams from the book *Cross-Functional Teams: Working with Allies, Enemies, and Other Strangers* by Glenn M. Parker (Jossey-Bass, 2003). The book is an easy read and full of examples, and my experience has been that the author's ideas and solutions work for the eventual problems that crop up in teams of OPM entrepreneurs and contacts provided by their partners.

vider with 75 to 80 percent, and you with 5 to 10 percent. This tactic usually has little impact on the partners' bottom line due to the small volume of the tests; the company doesn't have to make adjustments in its accounting system; and the costs of the test get buried in both companies' books. (In fact, in many cases the partner won't even bother to figure out what the costs were.) You receive a second benefit when you do the billing in the test stages; that process helps condition the partners to treat you as an independent agent who can buy and sell products or services, a conditioning that might help you negotiate the deal you want in your final agreements.

If the partners won't agree to billing through you, be sure to agree on who will bill the customers and collect revenue and then agree on how you and the partners will split revenue.

TIMELINES AND PRELIMINARY BUDGETS

Another important task is to make a timeline and a budget that list actions and responsibilities that your partners accept. You should take strong initiative here, leading the way to develop a timeline. One item you'll notice on the sample timeline that follows is *preorders*. A preorder is an order you get with just a prototype or small production run before you are actually ready to produce the product or service. Preorders are powerful tools in encouraging partners to move forward because they demonstrate that partners will be generating sales from the money they spend. List preorders whenever possible. The sample timeline and budget below is for a test market of a noiseless compressor for the dental industry that was originally mentioned in Chapter 3. After the table are comments about the action items to give you a better understanding of what the timetable is accomplishing.

Timeline for the Noiseless Compressor Market Test

Market: Northbrook, Illinois, high-rises; they contain in total seventy-five dental offices

Dealer Location: Hinsdale, Illinois

Participants: Patterson Dental, IronHorse Compressors, John Ludwig

Key Contacts: John Ludwig, Denny Swanson of Patterson Dental

Action Item	Responsible Party	Expected Costs	Date Completed
Receive preorder from Northbrook Associates and Smile Dentistry (selling price $7,500)	Swanson/ Ludwig	$0	June 1, 2006
Produce seven noiseless dental compressor systems	IronHorse Compressors	$28,000	August 15, 2006
Produce brochure and technical literature	Ludwig	$1,500	June 30, 2006
Mail out package about noiseless compressors to targeted offices	Ludwig	$750	June 30, 2006
Produce operations and maintenance manual	Ludwig/ IronHorse	$2,000	August 1, 2006
Complete initial calls on dental clinics to determine "hottest prospects"	Swanson/ Ludwig	$0	July 30, 2006
Demonstration/luncheon for dental clinics	Swanson/ Ludwig/ IronHorse	$3,000	August 15, 2006
Install two initial units at Northbrook Associates and Smile Dentistry	IronHorse/ Swanson/ Ludwig	$500	August 20, 2006
Obtain two additional orders for noiseless dental compressor systems	Swanson/ Ludwig	$0	September 30, 2006
Obtain three additional orders for noiseless dental compressor systems	Swanson/ Ludwig	$0	October 15, 2006

Timeline Comments

1. The target market has been carefully chosen to select a concentrated area with a high number of dentists in high-rise offices, who are the prime customers for a noiseless dental compressor, and to reflect the territory of just one Patterson Dental salesperson. That limits the scope of the operation.

2. The preorder for $15,000 is a good kickoff that justifies producing $28,000 worth of compressors.

3. The task of producing the compressors with a completion date of August 15 is listed before items that will be finished earlier, such as producing a brochure. That's because the work to build the compressor has to start before the brochures are completed. List items by start date rather than ending date.

4. The test project sells seven compressors because it is a fair number for the number of dentists' offices and because selling seven compressors will produce sufficient revenue to cover expenses in the market test period.

NINE

Preparing for a Win-Win Deal: Know What Everyone Offers and Needs

There are two or three parties, and sometimes more, in an OPM entrepreneur deal. The best deals are produced when everyone wins big, which starts with your understanding what everyone wants. Your goal is to have a chance to develop your ideas in a big way while making a small investment. You also want to protect your position and have some control over your business or product concept. The desires of marketers and providers are more complicated. A partner typically is more interested in how much a product will help the rest of the company. Marketers look for products that will help the sales of the rest of their line, and providers search for increased volume that can reduce their overall costs for their current volume. All potential partners will be evaluating both your idea by itself and your concept as it affects their entire business.

Remember as you are negotiating that you are searching for the win-win scenario for everyone. However, the win-win result is only partly from the OPM deal. Just as important is the situation the partner companies are in. The marketer needs to have lost marketing momentum for any number of reasons; the provider needs to have an underutilized production capacity. If companies are doing well, the deal is not as attractive to them. A tough negotiating partner may in fact be a partner who just doesn't need your deal desperately enough, and you may need to find another partner for whom your deal truly is win-win.

The goal of this chapter is to give you a firm understanding of what motivations lie beneath the surface for both marketers and providers. These issues easily get obscured in negotiation as all parties try for the best deal for themselves, but you need to understand just how much value everyone is bringing to the deal in order to look beyond the rhetoric and understand the potential partners' true positions so you get the best deal for yourself. This chapter will:

- Explain how OPM entrepreneurs position themselves for a win-win scenario
- Discuss what the marketing partner gains from a deal
- Show how the provider partner can have the most to gain, and why it is willing to put up much of the money
- Detail how long the deal should last
- Offer a list of key points to consider up front so they don't end up killing a deal later

A $200,000 PRODUCT LAUNCH

Sarah Alexander knew she had a great idea with kitchen wall racks that held ladles, stirrers, spatulas, and other long-handled kitchen items. She also knew that she couldn't afford start-up production costs, which—including inventory, operating costs, tooling, and fixtures—would probably run $200,000 or more. She approached a plastics manufacturer and suggested that they form a joint venture to put the product on the market. The manufacturer wanted to send out flyers to potential customers to check out the market's response. If they could land a major retailer, the manufacturer was willing to form a joint venture. So the flyers went out,

Alexander called all the big potential accounts, and she got one big customer committed to buying.

The manufacturer agreed to put up all the money, which ended up being closer to $300,000. Under their joint venture agreement Alexander received a small part of the profits and the manufacturer the rest until the manufacturer's investment was paid off. After the manufacturer got his money back, which took a little over two years, they split the profits fifty-fifty.

Why would the manufacturer agree to such a great deal for Alexander? The manufacturer's sales had been falling, and as a result its production wasn't producing enough profits to cover its expenses. The manufacturer was going to have to raise its prices to cover all of its overhead costs. That would make the company's prices noncompetitive, which would send the company into a death spiral. The company desperately needed new production to keep its costs down, and Alexander's product represented that opportunity. The $300,000 "loan" didn't matter because the kitchen racks were selling, and the owner knew that the money would come back in profits. The big benefit was that the manufacturer was able to cover its overhead without raising the prices on the rest of its product line, and the company was kept in a profitable business mode.

Note: In this example, Alexander chose to use big retailers as her marketing partner.

POSITIONING FOR YOUR WIN-WIN

Win-win includes a good deal for you, and that only happens if you end up with a strong share of the project's profits as well as profits from any derivative or peripheral products or services that are spawned from your idea. You don't want to be bought out for a sum of money, nor do you want a simple licensing deal in which you have no control and no benefit from the spinoff of additional products or services. Your partners are not going to just hand over a healthy share of the profits to you because they are good natured. They will do it because you've earned it.

You will succeed in getting a deal that's win-win for you when you bring four key elements to potential partners:

- A winning concept
- Low risk
- An identifiable path to the market
- Your ability to offer ongoing support

You want to constantly reinforce these four points with your partners as the project moves ahead to keep your position strong. The first two points, a winning concept and low risk, are important to sell early in the project, and we've discussed them earlier in the book. Packaging your concept was covered early on (Chapter 3) because you must not only have a winning idea; you also need to be able to package and present it to partners in a way that proves you have the professionalism needed to bring the deal off.

The last two points, a clear path to market and your ability to support the project, are the points that entice interested parties to sign the deal. They are also the two points that you need to prove to get your fair share of the project's ownership. You probably have covered these items earlier with your partners, because they are a part of what entices people to investigate your deal, but you shouldn't think the partners are completely sold on these points. You need to go back and hit these points firmly right before you attempt to negotiate your deal, or you could end up with a deal that leaves you with a minor position both for sharing the profits and for controlling the project.

The Path to Market

A *path to market* shows the complete product introduction process and how much time is left before introducing the product to the market. Doing a path-to-market presentation for partners is a convincing way for you to establish your value in the whole introduction process, to show how much work has been done, and to show how close you and the partners are to success. You could give a path-to-market presentation much earlier in the process, but in my experience it's better to wait and offer it right before the final deal, because its impact will be much less when closing a deal if you've shown it before.

Let's suppose that you say something like this to your partners: "I know you like the concept of _____, and the low risk associated with the project, but the big advantage I offer—and I hope you appreciate—is that I'm marshaling the resources available to bring the concept all the way to market. I've captured our introduction process, everything that's been accomplished to date, and how close we are to success. Our next step is to sign an agreement on how we will work together. But before discussing those terms, let's see where we stand on our path to market." That's a great opening statement. It establishes the primary role you have played up to this point—a much larger role than someone who just wants to sell or license a concept—and enhances your position to get the type of deal you want.

The path to market that you will show includes every step of the project, from inception to the final introduction. Don't make your path-to-market timeline too short; show the work that's been done and also show why you need to sign a deal now. The best path to market has some major event with a deadline to meet, such as a big convention or the start of a buying season. Without a deadline, projects can carry on indefinitely, and you definitely want to sign a deal. The path-to-market timeline that follows is an example of what you can show right before starting to negotiate for an agreement.

PATH TO MARKET

Product: The Broach Quick Jig, a new product for machining companies that improves productivity 20 percent when machining with broaches

Partner Companies: Sullivan Broach and Tool (marketing), Choung Machining (provider), Mark Colvin (concept developer)

Key Contacts: John Andreassen—Sullivan Broach and Tool; Denny Clarkson—Choung Machining; Mark Colvin

Date	Activity	Progress	Person Responsible
Nov 04	Create Concept	Complete	Colvin
Dec 04	Initiate documentation to protect patent rights	Complete	Colvin
Dec 04	Locate a machine company that can produce prototypes and eventual production	Complete	Colvin
Feb 05	Produce proof of concept model	Complete	Colvin/ Clarkson
Feb 05	Initiate internal test program	Complete	Colvin/ Clarkson
April 05	Modify proof of concept model, retest	Complete	Colvin/ Clarkson
May 05	Apply for patent	Complete	Colvin
May/June 05	Initial market feedback/users	Complete	Colvin
May/June 05	Initial market feedback/distributors	Complete	Colvin
June 05	Determine end-user-dictated price point	Complete	Colvin
June 05	Determine product has a 50%+ margin	Complete	Colvin/ Clarkson

June/July 05	Locate an established marketing partner	Complete	Colvin
July/Aug 05	Prepare three "looks like acts like" prototypes	Complete	Colvin/ Clarkson
Sept/Oct 05	Market test of prototypes with end users	Complete	Colvin/ Andreassen
Nov 05	Produce six additional broaches for market tests	Complete	Colvin/ Clarkson
Nov 05	Prepare operation instructions, price sheet, and one-page sales flyer	Complete	Colvin/ Andreassen
Nov 05/Feb 06	Offer test runs to potential customers in Greenville, South Carolina	Complete	Colvin/ Andreassen
Feb 06	Prepare report on the results of the market test	Complete	Colvin/ Andreassen
Mar/April 06	Sign agreements, commit resources, and prepare for market launch	Must be done by April 15 to hit deadline	Sullivan/ Choung/ Colvin
April 15, 06	Release orders to new tooling, order inventory	Order by April 15 to hit IMTS (International Machine Tool Show)	Clarkson
May 06	Prepare brochures and other sales collateral	Under development	Andreassen
June 06	Prepare promotional and initial sales plan	Under development	Andreassen/ Colvin

July 06	Prepare launch activities for IMTS	Under development	Andreassen/ Colvin
August 06	Have first production run, run tests at three sites to ensure tool's performance matches "looks like acts like" prototype	To be completed by August 15	Choung/ Colvin/ Clarkson
Sept 06	Product introduction at the IMTS show	Booth needs to be ordered by April 30	Colvin/ Andreassen/ Clarkson

You might think this product-to-market timeline looks too long and/or complicated. But your partners won't, especially if they are mid-size companies that are capable of selling or providing large quantities of your product. They will look at this timeline as just a summary, but the timeline still shows that this is your project, you have contributed heavily to the project's success to date, and deals need to be signed soon to hit a major introduction target.

PROJECTS ARE COMPLETED WITH LITTLE STEPS

Ron Nye was a thirty-year-old electrical engineer who was looking for a business to start. He knew several people who managed bars and restaurants, and they frequently mentioned that they might really make a bundle if they could cut back on the bartenders giving out free drinks or pouring drinks that were too big in order to receive bigger tips. Nye thought he could solve that challenge. "All" he needed was a spout for the liquor bottles that would pour a set amount of liquor into every drink and then send a wireless signal to the cash register to record the sale and to a central computer that would monitor liquor inventory. Nye thought the project was feasible, and bar owners said the system would be great, but in reality everyone thought the project was too complicated.

Nye first broke the project into components: the pouring spout; the sensor that determined when a drink was poured; the wireless chip to send a signal to the cash register; a wireless receiving unit on the cash register; an interface with the cash register's software; a wireless receiver on the computer used for inventory control; and then an interface with that computer's software.

Nye next went back to determine whether all the components were needed, and whether any of the components were too expensive for the value they provided. After several market interviews with both customers and engineers, he decided to drop the feature of linking with customers' inventory management systems. He also determined that configuring the cash registers could present a problem because there were just too many cash registers on the market to create a simple, cost-effective interface to work with all of them. So he decided to find a company with a leading-edge cash register system for bars and restaurants to be his marketing partner. The partner he finally chose also ended up handling the software programming to interface the wireless signals from the pouring spout to the cash register. His next step was to decide that liquor spout manufacturers were not a good choice as a provider; he instead decided to pursue a company in industrial measuring systems that used wireless technology. So Nye had a potential marketing partner (the cash register company) and a potential producing partner (the manufacturer of industrial measuring systems), and he had defined his own high-value role to play: coordinating installation and performing service and maintenance (which he actually did through a third firm.) Now it looked as though the project could be done, but people were still nervous. The partners decided to prepare a stripped-down model, with just one cash register, and to go to a trade show focused on the hospitality industry that was attended by owners of larger bars as well as owners and managers of restaurants, hotels, and resorts. Interest in the system was high, and one owner of sixteen restaurants that had large bar areas offered to have a unit put in for a test. If the system really worked, he would buy systems for at least five of his locations where he had significant problems with theft. Nye put together an action timeline with four or five checkpoints to be sure the job could be accomplished, and once they had a successful test they sold five units to launch the business. When he put together his path-to-market timeline, Nye showed that his value was unmistakable; he was resourceful and creative and able to overcome one significant challenge after another.

Continued Involvement

The last point to emphasize to your partners is that you are going to be working on the project full-time, or almost full-time, gathering market data, doing customer surveys, helping to find new markets, expanding the product line, and devoting your efforts to making the product a success. The example of Ron Nye's liquor monitoring system shows one way you can provide extensive value to partners. In Chapter 7, I outlined a series of roles OPM entrepreneurs can play that add value. Decide on your important role and use it to keep control of the project. Leading up to the final agreements, be sure to highlight both in your timeline and in discussions the role you've played and how important it is to the project's success.

Part of your responsibilities should be infiltration marketing: getting involved in the market and knowing what customers want today and in the future. As an infiltration marketer you are in the perfect position to continually suggest new derivative and peripheral products that will increase all partners' revenue streams and keep the partner companies as leaders in the market. This is really just an expansion of your role as an opportunity scout, but the benefit of this role should be stressed at this time, first because it emphasizes the role you've played to date in the project, and second because your role provides significant potential future value to the partners.

THE OUTSOURCE ENTREPRENEUR'S CUT

Splitting the profits or sales volume in any deal is a complicated negotiation that depends greatly on how much the manufacturer and marketer have to gain from the deal and how much each is willing or required to invest. Some points you should consider in negotiating your share of the profits:

- Standard royalty rates when you license a concept are between 2 and 6 percent of sales.
- Manufacturers or service providers typically won't do anything unless they receive a cut that covers their costs plus a 10 percent profit, and they will want to recover their total investment costs in twelve to eighteen months.
- Marketers will also want at least 15 percent of the sales price and sometimes up to 20 percent, depending on how much effort is required to sell the product.

In my opinion, the OPM entrepreneur must insist on a minimum of 10 percent of the sales price, or 25 percent of the profits, which is why projects need a margin of at least 40 percent; otherwise, no one will make enough money. This is also why the entrepreneur will try to run an OPM deal with just buy-and-sell agreements, which allows him or her to control her profit margin without partner interference, or try to get by with just one of the partners, with the OPM entrepreneur most often handling all of the marketing in order to increase her percentage of the profits.

Most outsource entrepreneurs at first believe they deserve an equal third of the profits, and maybe they do. But the problem is that manufacturers and marketers will believe they are doing most of the work and putting in most of the money. I have found that companies aren't willing to give equal shares to you. That's why you need to constantly sell your value and take the lead at critical project points with timelines and action lists to keep the project moving.

HOW MARKETERS GAIN

Marketers like a great new product, but they appreciate it mostly because it can help pull their entire product line along. Marketers want a product or service that will help them obtain more sales outlets, improve their product line, create a more complete customer solution, and help them expand into new markets. In an OPM entrepreneur project there are more people to split up the profits. Marketers might enter into an agreement if the sales potential is great even if your concept doesn't help their standard product line, but that isn't typically the case. It's up to the outsource entrepreneur to show how the marketer will benefit overall from the project.

More Sales Outlets

Most companies have product lines that aren't all that innovative and are subject to being pushed out of a distributor, retailer, or other sales outlet by a competitor that comes along with a better deal or a better promotion. Typically sales outlets like to limit their number of suppliers, so sales could drop throughout the marketer's entire product line if the competition has one product in its line that is superior to the marketer's product or service. The reverse is also true: a marketer with an innovative product will pick up sales in its ho-hum products when the sales outlet wants to carry the innovative product. Sales of the "me-too" products often fall to the supplier with just one or two innovative products.

The driving force behind any new product is that sales outlets will pick up an innovative product that customers really want. The most impressive thing you can do is to have interviews with sales outlets that buy from the marketer's competition, showing that those potential customers like the new product and are likely to buy it. You did some of these interviews early in the process when you prepared your initial presentation (Chapter 3), but those interviews typically deal with a product concept, as compared to the more finished version of the product or service that you should have developed by the time you are ready to sign a deal.

A More Complete Customer Solution

End users and those in the distribution channel do not like having to piece together products from different companies in order to form a complete solution for their needs. They are worried that some elements won't work right together and that their money will be wasted. Since confused or worried customers rarely buy, companies try to provide a complete solution for their potential customers. Again, the burden falls on you to get feedback from end users and market participants, now that your concept is developed, to verify that your product, in association with your partner's current products, does in fact present a complete solution.

MARKET REALITY

Marketers in "dog-eat-dog" competitive markets are always looking for an extra edge, which makes them prime OPM candidates. Cosmetic and beauty-care marketers face one of the toughest competitive markets, with demanding customers, lots of competitors, and a large number of new product introductions. Professional Solutions sold nail-care products to drug stores and supermarkets, places where shelf space often goes to the competitor with the best promotional deal.

—continued on next p

Expand into New Markets

Most products and services may be sold in one market but could have applications in others. Marketers in fast-growing markets will primarily be interested in strengthening their market position in their current market. But marketers in markets with slow or no growth look to new markets as a way to grow their business.

Again, with your concept developed, you need to get feedback in the new market that indicates your product or service is needed and that the distribution channel is excited about selling it. New markets present a tricky challenge. On the one hand, marketers are almost always willing to give the product a try in a new market if the costs are low. On the other hand, they don't have a strong marketing and sales infrastructure in place for that market to give the product a good chance to succeed. Your chances of a failed test rise dramatically when the marketer doesn't have an existing presence in a market, or doesn't know for sure what type of programs will work. You may need to take a leading role in creating an effective marketing plan before running into the market. You should be sure when going after a new market to have the partner assign someone to work with you to develop and implement that plan.

MARKET REALITY

—continued

Professional Solutions was all ears when it was approached by Michael Levin, who had created the Instant Nail Repair Kit based on his girlfriend's observation that there wasn't a product on the market that worked. Professional Solutions jumped on the idea and signed a private-label deal because it was confident the product could help it steal drugstore accounts away from its competitors. By far the most effective OPM sales proposition is the promise of improving the marketer's chances of becoming a prime supplier for distributors, retailers, or service companies.

If you haven't done a marketing plan before, you can use my book *Marketing Plan: Develop a Comprehensive Sales and Marketing Plan for Your Business, Service, or Product* (Adams Media, 2000) as a guide.

HOW PROVIDER PARTNERS GAIN

Manufacturers and service providers benefit the most from a deal because they get to spread their overhead costs over a larger number of products, a process that is called *excess overhead absorption*. This is the overwhelming reason that they will go into a deal. Chapter 5 (page 93) offers a complete explanation of overhead absorption, and you may want to refer to that discussion before approaching the provider partner to close the deal. Provider benefits are not limited to overhead absorption, though. You can also emphasize that the provider can establish a more stable revenue base and that the provider will have a more convincing sales presentation to prospective clients.

In many cases providers, especially providers that primarily do contract manufacturing or service work for other companies, don't have certainty about the volume they will be producing in the coming twelve months. A big customer today could be gone tomorrow. All providers are looking for more stable volume, which they can get from a product line or service of their own if they have one, or if they cooperate with an OPM entrepreneur in a partnership arrangement. Manufacturers also may be able to create a more powerful sales story if they participate in an OPM deal. A provider knows that producing a hot new product adds to the company's image and that the improved image will help it obtain business from other prospective customers.

HOW LONG FOR A WIN-WIN

The length of an agreement is of vital concern to the outsource entrepreneur. You need the deal to be for a minimum of three years, and preferably five, primarily because you will be in a weaker position when negotiating the deal for the second time and because you need to allow time for sales to develop to the point at which you can cash in.

When the deal is first struck will play a key role, and all the parties will feel that you are earning your keep. But after the partners have been involved in the deal for several years they will know the market, understand the customers fairly well, have ironed out most if not all of the start-up challenges, know the other partner and understand how to work together, and be aware of many, if not all, of the potential derivative or spinoff product features. All of this means that partners will have a greatly diminished view of your value at the two- to three-year mark of the venture, making it difficult for you to negotiate an agreement that is fair for you.

You also can't really cash in on your concept if the agreement is too short. The concept will be in the start-up mode for the first two years; with sales just developing, and with production ramping up, your income won't be overly high. You won't really start cashing in on an idea until year three, and you don't want a favorable agreement to expire before you receive a fair share of the profits.

Your agreement must be for a minimum of three years, but you really need to push for five. You may get resistance from the partners, but it is important that you hold firm. Your big selling point—and you may need to repeat this many times—is that you have spent lots of time developing the concept and putting everything together, and that you need at least five years to get a reasonable return. I wouldn't suggest going for more than five years, because you will then get really strong resistance. And in today's markets, few concepts can last more than five years anyway.

KEY POINTS TO CONSIDER

Several problems can arise that can derail your project pretty quickly, and you need to deal with these up front. Your potential partners won't even start contract negotiations if they feel it will be too difficult to come up with a fair deal, so you need to make sure that you understand their major concerns and that you let the partners know that these concerns will be covered in the upcoming contract. The partners will be much easier to negotiate with if your initial agreement proposals cover most of their concerns. Most of these concerns are more involved in three-way or joint venture agreements than they are in simpler two-way agreements or buy-and-sell agreements, but you still should understand the issues because the partners will want to cover these points somehow in their agreement.

1. *Recovering investments.* This can be an issue if your agreements require amortized start-up costs or if partners agree to equal investments to receive equal profit shares. Because projects typically don't require equal amounts of investment for marketing and

SUCCESS TIP

You should find out how your manufacturer calculates overhead before starting final negotiations with a provider. That knowledge will help you calculate just how much absorption each unit produces. For example, consider these conditions: the provider is a plastic injection molder; the overhead is based on a rate of $60 per machine hour; the provider can produce 600 pieces per hour; and the marketer has indicated it can sell one million units per year. The overhead absorbed by each part then is ten cents per piece, and the total overhead absorbed is $100,000. Those are facts that can seal the deal with the provider.

—*continued on next page*

production, you may need to have the project pay back a partner part of its investment from profits until all partners' investments are somewhat equal.

2. *Expenses versus investment.* Because your agreement may require that investments be reimbursed, you should establish what an expense is (expenses are not reimbursable), and what an investment is (investments *are* reimbursable). As a rule, no partner's time or employee's time is considered an investment, and minor expenses are just considered a normal part of doing business. Major costs or capital acquisitions exclusively for the business are considered investments. Tooling, equipment, ad campaigns, brochures, and trade-show expenses, if only for the project, may be considered investments.

3. *Investment approvals.* The investment to launch any project can be considerable, especially in working capital, which can easily be $250,000 to fund a $1 million-per-year sales level. Because an agreement may require amortizing the investment, or paying it back from the initial profit stream, you and the partners may want to approve investments. This can be a considerable sticking point if the partners have different

SUCCESS TIP

—continued

Typically, similar manufacturers absorb overhead in similar ways. A good way to find out how overhead rates are absorbed for your type of provider is to ask the suppliers of equipment to the manufacturer. If the manufacturer is in plastic injection molding, check the yellow pages for suppliers of plastic injection molded equipment; a salesperson for that supplier will probably tell you how overhead is typically absorbed. Information on service providers is more difficult to obtain, but you might have discovered this information in your initial questioning of providers.

investment philosophies (for example, if one wants to get by with minimal investments, while the other wants to have premier equipment). Include clauses in your agreements that require investments to be paid back and that require all parties to approve all investments.

4. *Not all income should pay investments.* Your partners may want to pay back everyone's investments before sharing profits, but that will leave you without any income. You want to stipulate that only 50 percent of the initial income pays back investments, with the remainder being split among the partners.

5. *Ownership when agreement ends.* When the partnership breaks up, it can be a problem deciding who owns the investments, especially if your agreement is for a short time. If that is the case, the partners should agree on a fair market value, or sell the equipment, and distribute the money based on each partner's share of profits. Disbursing investments can be tricky, especially because the investments with continuing value probably will all belong to the manufacturer. Disbursing investments is another selling point for a five-year agreement in which everyone can just keep the investments they have control of.

6. *Non-compete.* Partners should agree not to introduce a competing product for two to three years after the agreement ends without consent of the other party. This protects all the parties from someone leaving the partnership and going out on his own.

7. *Quality issues.* The product's quality affects everyone involved in the deal, and marketers will be concerned that they might have to market an inferior product. You will probably want to have all parties approve prototypes and drawings and to have first article inspection rights, which means that the parties have the right to review and approve the first products coming off the production

line. All parties should also have the right to approve production changes or any other manufacturing event that might change the product. The marketing partner might supply packaging, but all parties should have the right to review packaging in the same way they review production.

8. *Future funding.* If the project goes forward, future investments will be needed, probably by the manufacturer. When that need arises, the manufacturer might want other parties to share in the investment, or treat the investment as a loan with interest. The manufacturer will probably agree to front the investment with a prepayment schedule from profits if you discuss this up front.

TEN

Sign the Deal: Travel Any Road to a Successful Launch

Using the OPM approach doesn't require you to assume the same role on every deal. Instead, the entrepreneur can complete a deal using other people's money with a variety of approaches and roles. Your options for agreements range from actual joint ventures between two or three parties to your agreeing to sell your product or service on commission. Each type of deal has its pros and cons, and while you want the best deal available, you need to know all of the options to propose in order to keep negotiations moving along based on your and your partners' needs. The responsibility for framing the agreements so that they are favorable to everyone often falls to the OPM entrepreneur, which means you need to be prepared to suggest what you feel is the ideal structure and then to help structure the initial drafts of the agreements for your partners' approval before you approach an attorney.

The goal of this chapter is to help you understand your possibilities in structuring a deal. It is not intended that you become an expert on all the different types of contract arrangements you could use; instead, you should use this chapter to help set the framework of a deal that can be taken to a lawyer, who should draft the final agreement. This chapter will:

- Explain how to proceed based on your project's business value
- List the key considerations in every deal
- Show how to use multiple options to consider in a deal
- Include sample formats for supply, three-party, and joint-venture agreements

MIX AND MATCH

David French was an avid backpacker and camper who knew the frustrations of trying to cook on a trail in inclement weather. He developed the SureStart, a self-contained cooking system that would start in any weather. His product required products from two manufacturers: a cooking vessel that could both heat liquids and fry food, and a heating flux ring. French ran into his first challenge when he couldn't find a major marketing partner. He found that there were only small companies that sold niche market camping equipment products, and their volume wasn't enough to interest the manufacturers in investing to produce his product.

The only big companies servicing backpackers who had the volume that might entice a manufacturer to invest were ones that produced backpacking food. French approached a company that sold a popular brand of backpacking food carried by all the leading stores. The company wasn't interested in branching out into equipment. French knew, however, that the food company was introducing a new food line that worked extremely well in the SureStart. He suggested a special starter package, a combination of food and the SureStart, along with a contest, with ten winners receiving a free backpacking trip. The food company agreed, but only if it could buy the SureStart at 50 percent off French's proposed wholesale price.

French's second step was to talk to several of the largest manufacturers' sales agent groups in the market to see if they would carry the product once the six-month promotion was over. Once they agreed to carry the line, French went back to the manufacturers. He proposed making the initial order at no profit, using the order to pay for start-up manufacturing costs, with the manufacturers (and French) cashing in on subsequent orders to the market that would come through the rep groups. The manufacturers agreed to invest in the SureStart primarily based on their belief that the product would succeed with the initial market momentum generated by the first promotion with the backpacking food company.

French had an assortment of agreements to launch his product: a supply agreement at a greatly reduced cost to the backpacking food company; a three-way agreement between French and the two manufacturers to supply the product, specifying a price for the initial order, and then a price for subsequent orders; and supply agreements on a regionally exclusive basis to three manufacturers' sales agent groups.

A PROJECT'S BUSINESS VALUE

OPM entrepreneur projects range from opening the door to a lucrative long-term market, to introducing a product or service that can produce short-term revenue for the companies involved. To your partners, a project that opens up long-term business opportunities is more desirable, and they will be more interested in becoming involved. That allows you to potentially obtain a long-term position in a project that makes lots of money, but you'll also find that partner companies will be careful in such negotiations because they will want to protect their long-term position. Short-term deals, on the other hand, might not get partner companies as excited, but you can typically proceed with simple buy-and-sell agreements that are easy to execute and leave you with the most control.

The type of deal you will push for depends greatly on how your partners view the long-term value of your business opportunity.

Buy-and-sell agreements give you the most control but expire after a few years, while a joint venture might continue for ten years or more. For a big opportunity, the best way to protect your interest is a joint venture in which your share in the proceeds is guaranteed for up to ten to fifteen years.

Your concept has a high business value if it allows partners to enter a market poised for strong growth, competes in a large market, allows partners to gain rapid market share, or offers possibilities for many spinoff products or services. In any of these cases a concept provides a foundation for a strong, growing business. Opportunities like this do not come along very often, and potential partners will not want them to slip out of their control.

The Right Contract for High Value

Marketing partners in particular will want to control the concept if the opportunity has high business value. They will want to dictate product features, sales price, promotional efforts, and peripheral and derivative product development. They will probably not be willing to give you input regarding their decisions.

When the deal is big and the marketer or provider company wants control, you have to realize that the company has made a strategic business decision that this opportunity is important to its business future, which is why it wants to control the project. Nothing you can say is likely to change the company's mind. You can fight the company and possibly end up with nothing if the company decides you are too difficult to deal with, or you can strike a deal that will also benefit you long-term, even if you don't have as much control as you'd like.

The ideal situation for an OPM entrepreneur on a project with major potential, even if the marketer has total control of the project, is a joint-venture contract. A joint-venture contract gives you an ownership position in a company that could do well for years. The marketer and provider company might want a fifty-fifty joint venture, paying you a commission or other nonguaranteed return. You need to resist this arrangement, because the partners might be able to squeeze you out after a couple of years. The biggest advantage for you in a joint venture is that the venture will acquire value and could be bought out, or you could sell your share to one of the other partners. The drawback to you in a joint venture is that the partners might want to keep all the profits to reinvest in the business opportunity. In that case, you need to have the contract include a payment for some of your services, or a monthly contract payment.

A second choice for a project with big potential is a two- or three-party agreement. This is an agreement in which you and your partners agree to undertake certain responsibilities in launching your project. The agreement also spells out who will make which investments in the project and how the money received will be collected and disbursed. The major difference between three-party agreements and a joint venture is that each party carries out its responsibilities separately, and the parties do not form a separate legal entity to promote the product. Three-party agreements protect you with a deal that could last a long time. One drawback is that you don't have a separate legal entity to build up equity the way you do with a joint venture. If the marketer or provider wants control with a two- or three-party agreement, you can request compensation for giving up your control in a variety of ways, such as the following:

1. *A minimum payment of profit share that rises per year for five years.* Since you have less control, you shouldn't suffer if the marketing partner doesn't produce the expected results.

2. *A share for peripheral and derivative products.* You may not be in the best position to explore these opportunities if the marketer has control.

3. *A long-term agreement of at least five years.* Normally companies might want a three-year deal, but you should have a longer term in return for the loss of control, because it is unlikely that you will be able to negotiate a follow-up contract.

4. *Buyout provisions if the marketer fails to hit predetermined sales levels.* Again, if the marketer wants control, the marketer should have the responsibility to produce results.

Projects with Less Business Value

Your first choice is to use buy-and-sell agreements that give you ownership and control of the project. You can often get extended terms from the provider that will allow you to operate almost completely without any money of your own and still have complete ownership. Buy-and-sell agreements come with the entrepreneur's playing a wide variety of roles. You might want to refer back to Chapter 7, which goes through all the different roles you can play. The drawbacks to buy-and-sell agreements are that your partners can typically back out if things start out slowly, and you might not have strong rights to any peripheral or derivative products that your partners might develop.

The second choice, which reduces your control, is the two- or three-party agreement. A two- or three-party agreement gives you a deal that will last longer and is probably a better choice for projects that have solid if not spectacular potential. This kind of deal offers you a longer term than buy-and-sell agreements do, keeps your partners committed, and allows you to collect profits from peripheral and derivative products.

Susan Dyer loved to cook; she even attended chef classes so she could prepare gourmet meals at home. She also followed the marketing activities of the companies who compete in the gourmet cooking products market. The companies advertised in cooking magazines, put on trade shows and demonstrations in stores, and sent out huge mailings. While the companies were spending big dollars, Dyer's cooking friends took most of their advice from Web sites run by other cooking enthusiasts. Those sites didn't have the snazzy design features of a big company site, but they did have the information that cooks wanted for their next big meal.

Dyer felt that the kitchen supply companies were spending money without the results they were looking for, and that their lack of effectiveness offered an opportunity. She felt that the kitchen company Web sites were product rather than usage oriented, which cooks preferred. Dyer's concept was to deliver to a gourmet cooking products supply company an upscale Web site with the information that cooks wanted, a site that was patterned after the popular cooking tips sites and one that the supplier could sponsor. The supply company would benefit by building a database of visitors, having its name associated with a popular site, and having links to its home page for coupons, specials, and product information.

Dyer first lined up two providers, the creators of a cooking Web site and a Web design development firm. She had them prepare five sample pages and then approached the head of an advertising firm that did business with the largest gourmet cooking products supply company. Dyer signed Mutual Confidentiality Agreements with all parties, and when the deal went through she ended up with a 10 percent cut on all start-up and maintenance fees. Dyer purchased services from the two providers—the Web development and cooking Web site firms—and she sold the completed service to the advertising agency.

THE KEY ELEMENTS OF A DEAL

No matter how you structure an OPM deal, from buy-and-sell agreements to a full joint venture, there are certain elements that you must consider. Even if all of these elements aren't in formal agreements, you need to have clear understanding among all of the parties about how the elements are involved. If these elements are not in an agreement, I recommend that you send each party a letter outlining each point before you kick off the project. You can easily end up with misunderstandings and conflict between your partners if you don't address these issues up front. The sample buy-and-sell, three-party, and joint-venture agreements at the end of this chapter will also help you understand how to coordinate the key elements into an agreement. These elements should be spelled out in at least a few sentences for clarity. The following list contains a sample explanation for each element for the cooking Web site project mentioned earlier in this chapter. These explanations might be formatted into a letter to all parties. A letter to each party is especially important when separate buy-and-sell agreements are used that might not specify the overall working relationship.

1. *Marketing partner responsibilities.* The advertising agency is responsible for signing the gourmet cooking company to an agreement, helping to ensure that the site matches the company's marketing goals, providing links to the company's Web site, and initiating at least two company promotional programs that feature the Web site per year.

2. *Manufacturing partner responsibilities.* The cooking site information provider is responsible for biweekly updates to the site, featuring at least four new recipes or cooking techniques each time; major holiday features of at least ten new techniques to try; and stories about at least twelve new chefs per year. The Web

development company is responsible for Web page development, hosting, and maintenance, with a minimum of biweekly updates and a commitment of twelve hours per week for site maintenance, improvements, and adjustments.

3. *Role of the OPM entrepreneur.* The entrepreneur provides sales assistance and concept development with the advertising agency, interfaces with the cooking site and Web development provider, does weekly quality control checks on the site's operation, maintains the site's database, and monitors competitive activity at other cooking sites.

4. *Timing.* The initial presentation to the client will be in March 2006; a complete proposal with pricing will be delivered in April 2006, with projected start-up for the 2006 Christmas season on October 1, 2006.

5. *Investments.* All parties are responsible for the investments related to their respective activities.

6. *Expenses.* All parties are responsible for the expenses related to their respective activities.

7. *Revenue sharing.* All parties will deliver services at their costs plus their profit to the designated party—the Web site developer and cooking site developer to Dyer, and Dyer to the advertising agency.

8. *Peripheral or derivative products.* Dyer and the cooking site and Web page developers will be given right of first refusal on all additions or major modifications to the Web site. Dyer and the Web page developer will be given right of first refusal on other similar proposals from the advertising agency to its other clients for similar sites for other general interest groups such as gardeners, pet owners, or car enthusiasts.

9. *Operating strategy.* All agreements will be on purchase orders or supply agreements between the appropriate parties involved.

10. *Life of the agreement.* The purchase agreements will last for as long as the cooking site or any subsequent sites are operating.

11. *Ownership of intellectual property.* The copyrights for the cooking information will all belong to the cooking site information provider. The cooking site developer will not offer information sold to the advertiser to any other site or firm. In the event a book is subsequently published by the cooking site developer, all revenues will belong to the cooking site information developer.

12. *Dispute resolution and termination.* Each purchase agreement will contain its own independent clauses for termination for non-performance and, if applicable, independent clauses for dispute resolution.

OFFER MULTIPLE OPTIONS

You want to offer your partners an initial choice between buy-and-sell, three-party, and joint-venture agreements. Your preference is to have buy-and-sell or supply agreements that are easy to negotiate, and in most cases, you'll find that your business partners will also prefer simple agreements. They will only want more extensive agreements when they feel that the business concept has tremendous long-term value for them. The best approach with your partners is to use a simple dialogue, such as the one outlined in the next paragraph that recommends a buy-and-sell agreement. If your product has great business value, you might want to recommend a joint-venture or three-party agreement. The vast majority of the time you'll find that partners will accept the simpler agreements. Often they will even work with a purchase order, but you should request a supply agreement because you can include more protection for yourself in it.

A sample discussion might begin like this: "I think we are ready to proceed with a final agreement. I feel we could set up the deal with supply agreements, with the provider partners agreeing to supply to me, and then I agree to supply the marketing partner. We could also proceed with a three-way agreement or a joint venture. I personally feel the best approach, and the one that will by far be the easiest to negotiate, is to just proceed with supply agreements. Do you agree, or would you prefer another type of agreement?"

Once you get a commitment from the partners about the type of agreement they feel is most appropriate, tell them that you will prepare preliminary talking point agreements (all three sample contracts are talking point agreements) to ensure that all parties agree to the terms of the agreement before submitting the document to a lawyer for a final legal draft. All of the sample talking point agreements used in this section are based on the example of Susan Dyer and the cooking information Web site.

SUPPLY AGREEMENTS

Supply agreements are the easiest to negotiate, and they offer you the most control, but they also offer the most risk because you take title to merchandise. You could end up shipping a supply to the marketer and then learning that the marketer won't accept the supply or that it won't pay the bill. If that

OPM Entrepreneur Resources

Many of the contracts you can use in an OPM entrepreneurial deal are standard agreements. A site that contains a fairly complete list of legal agreement software is *www.tech-encyclopedia.com/ term/contract_management*. It has a list of twenty relatively easy-to-use software packages that you can use to create your own supply agreements.

happens, you still might be responsible for paying the provider. The following agreement tries to mitigate that risk by first stating that the cooking information needs to be approved by both the advertising agency and the cooking products supply company, and by stating that the payment terms to the provider are ten days after Dyer receives payment from the advertising agency. But there is still a risk that something could go astray when you have ownership of the product or service. If the risk is higher than you want to accept, consider a three-party agreement.

Supply Agreement

This Supply Agreement (Agreement) is made this 19th day of August, 2005 (Effective Date) between Dyer Communications, a Delaware Corporation, 1624 Fillmore Street, Minneapolis, MN 55411 (Dyer) and Gourmet Delight, an Illinois Corporation, 4890 Stoneybridge Avenue, Bellwood, IL 60104 (Gourmet).

1. Background.
    A. Dyer background: Dyer is a gourmet cook with a degree in communications and experience in marketing departments at several Minneapolis area companies. Dyer has developed a new concept for a loyalty marketing site for a major gourmet cooking products supplier that will help it create a stronger connection with its customers. Dyer's complete package is sold to the advertising firm, who then sells the Web site service to the cooking products supply company.
    B. Gourmet background: Gourmet created a gourmet cooking tips Web site in 2002 targeted at people who are just starting to explore their interest in gourmet cooking or

who are looking to further develop the gourmet cooking skills they currently have.

C. Purpose of Agreement. Dyer's loyalty marketing Web site requires biweekly updates with new interesting tips as well as major new sections related to holiday events. The purpose of this agreement is to contract with Gourmet to provide the information content for the Web site. Another firm, St. Cloud Web Productions, has been contracted to update the Web site in the proper format, and Gourmet only needs to provide informational copy and high-quality digital pictures.

2. Services.

A. Start-up materials. By June 1, 2006, Gourmet will supply information content for twenty-five to thirty Web pages with basic gourmet cooking tips, glossary of terms, links to other sites, and description of and uses for common gourmet cooking items.

B. Biweekly updates. Gourmet will provide four new cooking tips on a biweekly basis starting September 1, 2006.

C. Seasonal highlights. Gourmet will provide enough seasonal information for up to ten pages, including ten new recipes for Christmas, Easter, and the Fourth of July.

D. Featured chefs. Gourmet will supply a monthly feature on a major chef, with two or three cooking tips and one new recipe.

3. Separate Contract. Each delivery of information content shall stand as a separate and independent contract and payment shall be required for each shipment.

4. Approvals. Gourmet will furnish an initial set of materials to Dyer for approval by Dyer, the advertising agency, and the

cooking products supply marketing department by June 1, 2006. Subsequent biweekly updates, chef, and seasonal highlights must also be submitted for approval prior to payment. All materials to be delivered to Dyer's corporate address. Gourmet will have seven days to return corrected copy without incurring delivery days as cited in the penalty clause provision of this Agreement.

5. Fees.
   A. Start-up materials $25,000
   B. Biweekly updates $2,000
   C. Seasonal highlights $12,500
   D. Chef highlights $5,000

6. Penalties. Prices will be reduced by ten percent for each week content is late.

7. Terms. Payment is due from Dyer to Gourmet ten days after Dyer receives payment from the advertising agency.

8. Warranties. Gourmet warrants that its delivered original content will not infringe on any copyrights, or have been previously published unless agreed to by Dyer, the advertising agency, and the cooking products supply company. It is understood that some of the basic set-up content relating to equipment and basic cooking tips may be similar to information previously published on Gourmet's own Web site.

The foregoing warranties are exclusive and are given and accepted in lieu of any other warranties, expressed or implied. The remedies to Dyer shall be limited to those provided in this agreement.

9. Restrictions. Gourmet agrees not to enter into a separate agreement with any other parties to provide cooking product information for a period of twelve months after the termination of this Agreement.

10. Confidentiality. Both parties agree to abide by the Mutual Confidentiality Agreement attached as Appendix A to this Agreement.

11. Term. This agreement shall be for the period that the cooking products supply company agrees to pay for the Web loyalty site on cooking products. Restrictions listed in paragraph 10 of this Agreement shall survive for three years after termination of this Agreement.

12. No Assignment. This Agreement and any rights created by it cannot be assigned by either party without the other party's prior written approval.

13. Termination. The Agreement can be terminated by Dyer if Gourmet fails to produce information that meets with the approval of Dyer, the advertising agency, or the cooking products supply company. Gourmet may terminate agreement if Dyer is more than sixty days late with payment for services provided. Prior to termination the party terminating must provide a letter of concern to the other party and the other party has fifteen days to remedy the complaint of nonperformance. The obligations of confidentiality set forth in this Agreement shall survive termination of this Agreement.

14. Entire Contract. The Agreement between Dyer and Gourmet in connection with the services and goods identified in this Agreement supersedes all previous communications, representations, and agreements, oral or written, between the parties with respect to the services and goods in this Agreement.

15. Governing Law. This Agreement is governed by the laws of Minnesota.

IN WITNESS THEREOF, the parties hereto have caused this Agreement to be executed as of the Effective Date first set forth above.

For Dyer

Dated: _____   _____

Susan Dyer, President

For Gourmet

Dated: _____   _____

Ann Joyner, President

THREE-PARTY AGREEMENTS

Three-party agreements don't expose OPM entrepreneurs to as much risk as do supply agreements, since title of the product or service typically passes from the provider to the marketer, with the OPM entrepreneur getting a share of the provider's proceeds. Three-party agreements are in a way a partnership or a joint venture, but there are significant differences. A partnership or joint venture is a new legal entity; a three-party agreement is not, and as a result a three-party agreement is easier to set up and maintain. Another difference is that the revenues are collected by the partnership or joint venture, which is a separate legal entity with each partner owning a share, and then profits are split based on each party's ownership share of the joint venture or partnership. In a three-party agreement, one of the parties collects revenue and then disburses monies to the other parties. Three-party agreements require specific clauses that explain how and when money is disbursed from the party receiving the money to the other parties. Because they are simpler to set up and maintain, most OPM entrepreneur partners will prefer a three-party agreement. Joint-venture agreements are only used when the concept presents major profit and revenue opportunities for the parties and when significant investments are required to capitalize on those opportunities.

For this agreement Christy Advertising, Gourmet Delight, and Dyer Communications are the three parties. Dyer has a separate contract with the Web development firm and therefore, in this agreement, Dyer takes on all the responsibilities of Web development.

Three-Party Agreement

Gourmet Cooking Tips and Products Web Site

This Three-Party Agreement (Agreement) is made this 19th day of August, 2005 (Effective Date) between Dyer Communications, a Delaware Corporation, 1624 Fillmore Street, Minneapolis, MN 55411 (Dyer), Gourmet Delight, an Illinois Corporation, 4890 Stoneybridge Avenue, Bellwood, IL 60104 (Gourmet), and Christy Advertising, a California Corporation, 15935 Nordhoff Street, Suite 220, Los Angeles, CA 90022 (Christy).

1. Overview.
    A. Dyer background: Dyer is a gourmet cook with a degree in communications and experience in marketing departments at several Minneapolis area companies. Dyer has developed a new concept for a loyalty marketing site for a major gourmet cooking products supplier that will help create stronger connections with its customers. Dyer has contracted with an established Web development firm with experience in creating sites for large consumer products companies, and Dyer has experience interfacing with Web development firms to create Web sites with high consumer appeal.
    B. Gourmet background: Gourmet created a gourmet cooking tips Web site in 2002 targeted at people who are just starting to explore their interest in gourmet cooking or

who are looking to further develop the gourmet cooking skills they currently have.

C. Christy background: Christy has been the advertising agency for the target gourmet cooking products supplier for seven years and has created the company's branding strategy, look, and marketing and promotional materials. It has gained the cooking products supplier's trust and is responsible for developing a loyalty marketing program for the cooking products supplier.

D. Purpose of Three-Party Agreement: Prepare and maintain a high-quality loyalty Web site for the cooking products supplier that features cooking tips, product information, biweekly updates, features on leading chefs, and seasonal cooking feature sections.

E. Timing: Introduction of loyalty Web page concept to gourmet cooking products supplier in March 2006, with an October 1, 2006, Web page start-up.

2. General Description of Responsibilities.

A. Dyer: Provide sales and concept assistance to Christy, interface with Gourmet regarding information format, and manage the Web development firm that will provide start-up Web development, ongoing maintenance, and a quarterly upgrade to the site's performance.

B. Gourmet: Prepare informational content for general site information including descriptions of common gourmet techniques and cooking products; biweekly updates with new recipes and techniques; monthly features on established and up-and-coming chefs; and major holiday information packages.

C. Christy: Present and sell the loyalty Web page concept to the gourmet cooking products supply company, assist

Dyer in the preparation of five or six Web pages of presentation materials to ensure that they match the look and feel of the cooking products company's marketing materials, and assist Dyer and Gourmet to prepare the initial Web site materials and subsequent updates, ensuring the site matches the company's standard look. Christy has final approval of the materials presented to the cooking products supply company, both for the initial presentations and then for subsequent updates.

3. Investments. Each party is responsible for their investments.

4. Expenses. Each party is responsible for their expenses.

5. Revenue Sharing. Christy will receive income for the loyalty Web site; the proceeds from the Web site will be twenty percent to Christy, forty percent to Gourmet, and forty percent to Dyer payable quarterly 39 days after the end of the quarter.

6. Pricing. Parties will each have a vote on pricing decisions, with agreement of two out of three parties sufficient to set prices.

7. Site Development and Design. Initial Web page design and layout provided by Dyer, but Christy has final approval for the site's design. Dyer to complete Web site changes requested by Christy.

8. Peripheral and Auxiliary Products. Each party shall offer the right of first refusal to the other parties on any subsequent loyalty Web page business concepts developed by any of the parties, including major modifications to the current site, new cooking tip sites, or Web tips related to other topics.

9. Operating Strategy. Christy will solicit orders and collect start-up, monthly maintenance, holiday, and major site modification

fees, and then distribute fees as described in the revenue sharing description in this Agreement. Gourmet and Dyer will complete start-up, monthly upgrades, and seasonal highlights per the work schedule listed in the Agreement.

10. Work Timetable:
   A. Start-up materials: Gourmet, have initial materials prepared sixty days after signing cooking products supply company; Dyer, have content on a preliminary Web page design thirty days after receiving materials from Gourmet.
   B. Biweekly updates: First set from Gourmet, 120 days after signing; Dyer, complete site work fourteen days after receiving materials from Gourmet. Every two weeks thereafter for both Gourmet and Dyer.
   C. Seasonal highlights: Gourmet, 120 days prior to holiday; Dyer, thirty days after receipt of materials from Gourmet.
   D. Chef highlights: Gourmet, 150 days after signing; Dyer, fourteen days after receiving materials from Gourmet.

11. Warranties. Gourmet warrants that its delivered original content will not infringe on any copyrights, or have been previously published unless agreed to by Dyer, Christy, and the cooking products supply company. It is understood that some of the basic set-up content relating to equipment and basic cooking tips may be similar to information previously published on Gourmet's own Web site.

The foregoing warranties are exclusive and are given and accepted in lieu of any other warranties, expressed or implied. The remedies to Dyer and Christy shall be limited to those provided in this Agreement.

12. Restrictions. Gourmet, Dyer, and Christy agree not to enter into a separate agreement with any other parties to provide cooking product information for a period of twelve (12) months after the termination of this Agreement.

13. Intellectual Property. The copyrights for the cooking information on the site all belong to Gourmet. Gourmet will not offer information furnished as a part of this Agreement to any other site or firm. Gourmet will retain the rights to publish the cooking tips in book form and will retain all the income from any such published book.

14. Confidentiality. All parties agrees to abide by the Mutual Confidentiality Agreement attached as Appendix A to this Agreement.

15. Term. This Agreement shall be for the period that the cooking products supply company agrees to pay for the Web loyalty site. Restrictions listed in number 12 of this Agreement shall survive for three years after termination of this Agreement.

16. No Assignment. This Agreement and any rights created by it cannot be assigned by any party without both of the other parties' prior written approval.

17. Termination. A party's participation in the Agreement can be terminated by agreement of the other two parties if it fails to perform the functions specified in this Agreement. Prior to termination, the parties terminating must provide a letter of concern to the other party, and the other party has fifteen days to remedy the complaint of nonperformance. The obligations of confidentiality set forth in this Agreement shall survive termination of this Agreement. The terminating parties must provide the departing

party 25 percent of its expected revenues over the twelve months after termination.

Any of the parties may withdraw from the Agreement with six months' notice to the other parties.

18. Entire Contract. The Agreement between Dyer, Gourmet, and Christy in connection with the services and goods identified in this Agreement supersedes all previous communications, representations, and agreements, oral or written, between the parties with respect to the services and goods in this Agreement.

19. Governing Law. This Agreement is governed by the laws of Minnesota.

IN WITNESS THEREOF, the parties hereto have caused this Agreement to be executed as of the Effective Date first set forth above.

For Dyer
Dated: _____   _____
                                            Susan Dyer, President

For Gourmet
Dated: _____   _____
                                            Ann Joyner, President

For Christy
Dated: _____   _____
                                            Janet Christy, President

JOINT-VENTURE AGREEMENT

Joint ventures or partnerships are separate companies, potentially with their own management, financial control, and frequently their own operating divisions. Setting up joint ventures calls for an investment or loan for operating capital alone, and the legal fees and administrative headaches of setting up a joint venture can be substantial. Typically most of your potential partners will shy away from a joint venture unless it represents a major business opportunity. Shown below is a joint-venture agreement for the same three parties as the three-party agreement for the cooking tips and products Web site. A partnership agreement, which is occasionally used by smaller companies, is similar to a joint venture; you can use this same format in the draft legal document and then let your attorney draw it up as a partnership agreement.

This particular joint venture agreement has a limited scope and includes an administrator that is controlled by the votes of the three parties. Most joint ventures will have independent management and a board of directors. Typically each involved party will be allocated seats on the board to protect their operations. This joint-venture agreement also has the parties buying services of the employees from the provider partners. A larger joint venture would probably have employees from each partner assigned to it, often working as employees of the joint venture, to complete their assignments.

This joint-venture agreement solves the OPM entrepreneur's problem of needing money on an ongoing basis by having the joint venture pay each partner for the services rendered within thirty days.

Joint-Venture Agreement

This Joint-Venture Agreement (Agreement) is made this 19th day of August, 2005 (Effective Date), between Dyer Communications, a Delaware Corporation, 1624 Fillmore Street, Minneapolis, MN 55411 (Dyer), Gourmet Delight, an Illinois Corporation, 4890 Stoneybridge Avenue, Bellwood, IL 60104 (Gourmet), and Christy Advertising, a California Corporation, 15935 Nordhoff Street, Suite 220, Los Angeles, CA 90022 (Christy)

1. Overview.
    A. Business Purpose. The business of the Joint Venture is to prepare, market, and maintain a loyalty Web site for cooking tips and products for a gourmet cooking products supply company.
    B. Term of the Agreement. This Joint Venture shall commence on the date first above written and shall continue in existence for at minimum the length of time the loyalty Web site continues in operation.

2. Definitions.
    A. Affiliate. An affiliate of an entity is a person that, directly or indirectly through one or more intermediaries, controls, is controlled by, or is under common control of such entity.
    B. Capital Contribution(s). The capital contribution to the Joint Venture actually made by the parties to the Joint Venture, including property, cash, and any capital equipment.

C. Profits and Losses. Any income or loss of the Joint Venture for federal income tax purposes as determined by the Joint Venture's fiscal year.

3. Management. The three parties will appoint a financial controller from Christy to manage the Joint Venture activities (the Administrator), with all major decisions determined by majority votes of the three parties, with each party having equal votes. The Administrator shall have authority to sign documents and checks and commit the Joint Venture to contracts and other obligations subject to direction from the Joint Venture parties.

4. Capital Contributions. Christy will fund the Joint Venture with a $50,000 loan; the loan will be paid back from operating profits prior to any distribution of profits as outlined in this Agreement.

5. Operational Strategy. Gourmet and Dyer will perform work for the joint venture, billing the joint venture at seventy-five dollars per hour for work performed. Christy will be paid 10 percent sales commission by the Joint-Venture on all revenues received.

6. Profit and Loss Distribution. Commencing on the date hereof and ending on the termination of the business of the Joint Venture, all profits and losses shall be distributed sixty days after the conclusion of each fiscal year at the following percentages: Christy–sixty percent; Gourmet–twenty percent; Dyer–twenty percent.

7. Duties of Parties.
   A. Christy: Administrate the Joint-Venture; provide personnel to handle the sales and customer service; interface with the cooking supply products company, in return for a 10 percent sales commission; provide input into the

Web site content and design; and provide artwork and copy required to match the Web site to the cooking products supply company's other promotional efforts.

B. Dyer: Provide Web site design, maintenance, and upgrades in return for seventy-five dollars per hour; provide sales assistance to Christy; offer input to the overall effectiveness of the site at no additional charge.

C. Gourmet: Provide Web page content for basic gourmet cooking techniques and products, biweekly updates, chef interviews, and seasonal holiday cooking tips and recipes in return for seventy-five dollars per hour for preparation time.

8. Other Business of the Parties to This Agreement. The parties to this Agreement and their respective Affiliates may have interests in businesses other than the Joint Venture business. The Joint Venture shall not have the right to the income or proceeds derived from such other business interests.

9. Payment of Expenses and Fees. All expenses of the Joint Venture and all invoices for services rendered by Dyer and Gourmet shall be paid by the Administrator within fourteen days of receiving an invoice.

10. Confidentiality. All parties agree to abide by the Mutual Confidentiality Agreement as attached as Appendix A to this Agreement. The terms of confidentiality apply for twenty-four months after the dissolution of this Agreement.

11. Indemnification of the Parties. The parties to this Agreement shall have no liability to the other for any loss suffered which arises out of any action or inaction if, in good faith, it is determined that such course of conduct was in the best interests of

the Joint Venture and such course of conduct did not constitute negligence or misconduct.

12. Dissolution. The Joint Venture shall be dissolved upon the happening of any of the following events:

A. Bankruptcy. The adjudication of bankruptcy, filing of a petition pursuant to a Chapter of the Federal Bankruptcy Act, withdrawal, removal, or insolvency of any of the parties.

B. Sale. The sale or other disposition, not including an exchange of all, or substantially all, of the Joint Venture assets.

C. Mutual agreement of the parties.

13. Total Agreement. This Agreement constitutes the entire understanding and agreement among the parties hereto with respect to the subject matter hereof, and there are no agreements, understandings, restrictions, or warranties among the parties other than those set forth in this Agreement.

14. Notices. All notices to parties shall be in writing and shall be deemed to be delivered when deposited in the United States mail, postage prepaid, certified or registered mail, return receipt requested, and addressed to the parties at their respective addresses set forth in this Agreement or at such other addresses as may be subsequently specified by written notice.

15. Governing Law. This agreement is governed by the laws of Minnesota.

16. Other Instruments. The parties agree that they will execute each such other and further instruments and documents as are or may become reasonably necessary or convenient to effectuate and carry out the purposes of this Agreement.

IN WITNESS THEREOF, the parties hereto have caused this Agreement to be executed as of August 19, 2005.

For Dyer

Dated: _____   _____

                                    Susan Dyer, President

For Gourmet

Dated: _____   _____

                                    Ann Joyner, President

For Christy

Dated: _____   _____

                                    Janet Christy, President

ELEVEN

REVERSE THE TABLES: ENCOURAGING ENTREPRENEURS TO KEEP BRINGING YOU DEALS

The OPM entrepreneur approach works because it provides benefits to the marketing and manufacturing partners. OPM entrepreneur projects help minimize the risk of an idea failing. They also provide, free of charge until sales are made, a gung ho, hard-working entrepreneur who helps push the project forward. Marketing or manufacturing companies who want to take advantage of the opportunities provided by OPM entrepreneurs can increase their chances by finding individuals or small companies positioned to play that role and then encouraging them to find projects and opportunities in the company's market or industry.

Marketing companies often are in the best position to drive this process. They may have a general idea of what customers need or want, or what trends might be coming, so they will recognize that a particular concept might have potential. They might need the help of an OPM entrepreneur, however, because they may not know the customers' specific needs and wants well enough to create a winning product or service specification. Even if they can define the customers' needs, they may not know how to get the product or service produced, or where and how to find a company willing to invest in production. For example, in the case of my latest project, which is marketing a diesel particulate filter from Denmark in North America (see Introduction, pages xiii-xiv) a company in the business told me that it knew the market needed a more durable diesel particulate filter. However, it didn't know what that product should be like or where to obtain it, nor did it have the resources to fund a new manufacturing start-up. The company asked me for help. I was able to make the connections with a manufacturer capable of delivering the right product and willing to make the investment required to produce the product for the North American market.

Manufacturers often have the reverse situation. They may think they have a product that could solve a problem, but they might not have access to the detailed market intelligence that an OPM entrepreneur can produce to create a winning product, or they might not know how to connect with marketing companies capable of taking the product to market in a major way. The manufacturing company that I'm currently dealing with thought it might have a solution to the problem of diesel emissions for the North American market, but it didn't completely understand the market and didn't have a marketing partner to help it define exactly what the product should be like in North America or how to sell the product in the face of required regulatory approvals. The company was happy to work out a deal when I called, and everyone ended up a winner.

Potential partner companies can find helpers the same way entrepreneurs do, by going to association meetings and trade shows. While at those meetings and shows they should take the time to meet people from small companies, consultants to the industry, manufacturers' representatives, and technical experts from universities. Companies can nurture these relationships by talking with these contacts about new developments, market trends, and what the contacts would like to see companies do in the market. With enough contacts, companies should be able to encourage someone to step up to lead the project in return for making their cut on the final deal.

The goal of this chapter is to encourage the OPM entrepreneur approach from both sides of the street: projects that the OPM entrepreneur starts, and projects that partner companies suggest to potential OPM entrepreneurs. If you are working for a company, you'll learn how projects that you can't do on your own can become a reality if you pursue an OPM entrepreneur relationship. Partner companies might not make as big a percentage as they would if they did the projects themselves, but often an OPM entrepreneur approach is the only way they can participate in the launch of a promising project. This chapter will:

- Explain how to find potential OPM entrepreneurs
- Discuss how companies can develop relationships with candidates likely to become involved in OPM entrepreneur projects
- Offer guidelines and suggestions to help partner companies encourage an individual to become an OPM entrepreneur
- List the characteristics of projects you might offer an OPM entrepreneur

WHY SO LONG

For four or five years BlackBerry offered the only mobile e-mail solution that didn't require carrying around your computer. Black-Berry was geared toward business executives needing advanced capabilities and it was fairly expensive, for both the hardware and the monthly service fee.

At the same time there were other hand-held devices on the market, including Palm Pilot, Symbian, and Windows Mobile, but they didn't provide e-mail services. Cell phones started adding simple text messaging services, which were great for individuals but didn't hold the typically longer business message. Finally a company called JP Mobile began offering e-mail service, with similar features to the BlackBerry but that worked with other hand-held devices, for $12.95 per month. JP's service doesn't require any additional software, and it is easy to start up for new users. JP Mobile provides a great solution for small companies with people on the go and even for individuals who want more communication than a simple text message when they are away from home.

The question is: Why did it take so long to come out with a service for other hand-held devices to compete with the Black-Berry? This was great business for wireless companies, a big asset to the other hand-held devices on the market, and a real service to end users who were looking for a less expensive alternative to a BlackBerry. The technology to create a new mobile e-mail system wasn't that difficult, and therefore the product could have been on the market much sooner. The reason for the delay is that the new product required skill sets from several companies: the other hand-held device manufactures; a software development team; and the wireless network of established wireless suppliers. Coordination of many companies is a skill that companies often lack, which is exactly the role that an OPM entrepreneur can pull off. When a "crazy, hare-brained" entrepreneur comes in with a new opportunity, most companies will shy away, not wanting to waste their time. Those companies will often be late responding to market opportunities, and will settle for minor market positions. Other, more innovative companies will welcome the entrepreneur to see just what he is proposing. That entrepreneur might offer the quickest way to cash in on a market opportunity in a big way.

FINDING POTENTIAL OPM ENTREPRENEURS

If you work for a manufacturer or marketer you probably see a new trend or market need on a fairly regular basis, at least once a year. Often you may not be able to act on that knowledge. The reasons you can't act are many, and may include these:

- The company is too busy with other projects.
- The project is too expensive for the company's resources.
- The product isn't the right manufacturing fit.
- Your company doesn't have a sales and marketing distribution network in the target market.

In such a situation, you have four choices for moving ahead: do nothing, try to convince your management to change their mind, hope an OPM entrepreneur approaches you, or find someone with an entrepreneurial bent and encourage him or her to take on the project as OPM entrepreneur.

You are not looking for individuals from major corporations, but rather individuals who work independently or in a very small company, or who sell on commission. Every industry I've belonged to is full of individuals who qualify. They include consultants to the industry, sales representatives and writers for trade magazines, manufacturers' representatives, people who import one or two products, individuals from small companies that provide a service, salespeople who work on commission from a distributor, and technical experts from universities or independent testing laboratories. If you work for a mid-size to large company, you've probably never noticed how many of these targeted OPM entrepreneurs are in your industry. Most markets or industries have at least twenty-five individuals who could be an OPM candidate, and many have more than a hundred.

These target contacts will know the market and are already at least somewhat entrepreneurial. More important, they will be able to take on the initial work of a new OPM deal, and may even be able to run the entire deal, while still keeping alive their current source of income. They aren't tied to a company job for forty to fifty hours per week; instead, they have freedom in their employment and are able to spend time developing the project, working at night or weekends if necessary to catch up on their other work. Their risk is low because they aren't giving up a job to pursue an opportunity, and if the opportunity doesn't pan out, they can keep doing what they were doing when you first suggested they look into an OPM deal.

Finding the contacts you need to explore your idea isn't difficult, because these individuals are approaching companies like yours all the time to sell them products or services. They are especially likely to attend trade shows or association meetings. When you go to a trade show or association event, take the time to meet people you might target for an OPM approach. This means talking to people at breaks, spending time in the refreshment areas talking to new people, being open to an individual who wants to know more about your business, and serving on as many committees as you have time for. You should also accept appointments in your office from consultants or trade magazine personnel when they call to see you, even if you don't have any business to offer them. You especially want to see people who call you with business proposals to exploit a new market, because they may already be venturing into the OPM entrepreneur arena. These are the people you want to encourage to explore an OPM deal. You'll find some individuals who are bright and creative and looking for ways to move the industry ahead. You should nurture relationships with promising people so that you can talk to them about new developments and market trends and what they'd like to see done in the market.

DEVELOPING RELATIONSHIPS

You should cultivate relationships with your top three or four candidates for an OPM project. This is a good business practice even if you never proceed with an OPM project, because you've identified these individuals as astute, creative people who are involved in the same market and industry as you are. They have insights into the market changes that can help you stay on the leading edge of the market with new products and services. You also want to develop the relationship so that when you have an idea for a project your company can't do alone, one for which you need an OPM entrepreneur, you'll have contacts to entice into playing the role of the entrepreneur in return for a share of the eventual profits. Effective ways to nurture your relationships are phone calls, meetings for dinner or coffee at trade shows and association meetings, hosting an advisory council, and using contacts for sales meetings and other events.

During your phone calls and dinner meetings you should explain to the contacts your company's need to explore partnerships and other relationships in the market to stay ahead of the competition. You can explore with the contact the motivations behind and the activities of other partnerships in the industry, and the moves other companies have made regarding partnerships, alliances, and joint-cooperation agreements. Explain that your company has limited resources and that in order for your company to move ahead you need to look into how you can leverage your efforts with the efforts of others. Ask the contact for suggestions about what type of alliances could benefit you, and who potential partners might be.

Advisory councils can be formal or informal depending on your company size. You might just meet with your council members at trade shows for a dinner, or you might bring them into your company headquarters for a day, paying their expenses as well as a stipend for coming and offering direction. You can pose the same types of discussions with your advisory council as you do in individual meetings, such as how to create partnerships or other innovative tactics to greatly expand your company's sales. Depending on the group dynamics, advisory councils can work better or worse than individual meetings. They work better when the members of the group feed off each other's ideas and come up with more innovative suggestions; they work worse if the group is dominated by one member or if people won't speak freely in a group.

A last tactic is to bring in your contacts, paying expenses and a stipend, to make presentations to your board members, sales staff, distributors, or key contacts about the state of the industry and where it is going. You can also invite these people to events you might sponsor at industry association meetings or trade shows, or at regional or local events that cater to your key customers. I have found that using contacts for presentations and events enhances the relationship tremendously because it establishes that you value the input and trust the judgment of your contact.

NOBODY MOVES FASTER

In late 2003, U.S. newspapers had small articles stating that at the beginning of 2004 Singapore was going to lift its ban on chewing gum. It was a trivial fact that most people probably ignored, but it caught Art Baer's attention. He flew to Singapore, talked to government officials, and learned that the government wanted citizens to chew gum to fight tooth decay. He received a list of the government's requirements, which no current gum met, and found a manufacturer who could make the gum to the government's specifications. He then found a sales and marketing company that sold products to Singapore's drugstores, and he got his product into stores six weeks before Wrigley's did. Being first had its merits: Baer's company, Impress Gum, held 40 percent market share after a year on the market.

Baer's project would have been considered a wild-goose chase by most companies. Drop everything and go to Singapore? Most companies wouldn't think it was worth the expense of a trip. Singapore was just a small part of the worldwide chewing gum market. But to Baer, a tax-deductible trip to Singapore for a chance to set up a business that could pay him $100,000 or more per year didn't seem like such a bad idea; in fact, it was downright appealing. For many companies that's the beauty of an OPM deal; you can use an

OPM entrepreneur to check out an opportunity that you can't or choose not pursue. The cost of the initial groundwork is all at the OPM entrepreneur's risk. If the deal goes through you'll still make money, and if doesn't you don't lose out. The OPM entrepreneur also wins, as he or she can land a $100,000-plus yearly income for a small investment in an idea for which the entrepreneur already has one potential partner eager to be a part of an OPM deal.

ENCOURAGING POTENTIAL OPM ENTREPRENEURS

If you feel you may need someone to step into an OPM role for you, start by keeping track of all the activities that are close to OPM deals in your market or industry, because you can use them to demonstrate to a potential OPM entrepreneurial candidate that the industry is receptive to an OPM approach. The types of activities you want to track include entrepreneurial middleman deals, contract manufacturing agreements, and private-label arrangements.

An entrepreneurial middleman can be an importer who brings in parts from overseas and then sells to distributors or other marketers; a service broker who finds the right service person to maintain or fix equipment; and a master distributor that takes all of a company's production and then has it sold by a network of local or regional distributors. All that counts is that the middleman is the fulcrum for joining together two companies to put a product or service into the market.

An industry with active contract manufacturers who agree to produce a product designed and then sold by another company is an industry open to OPM entrepreneur deals, because many products are already being brought to market with partners and alliances. Private-label deals are of interest because they might be from an inventor who arranges for a manufacturer to produce the product, which is then sold under a private-label agreement by a marketer. Private-label deals from inventors are frequently done on an OPM basis. At other times, private-label deals are struck by marketers who have a product concept and find a manufacturer to produce it—again, a type of alliance and partnership in which companies work together to put the product on the market.

OPM ENTREPRENEUR RESOURCES

OPM entrepreneurship is a result of major market shifts due to major changes in technology and customer needs. Companies both big and small have responded with multiple partnerships and alliances. The book *The Entrepreneurial Mindset* by Ruth Gunther McGrath and Ian MacMillan (Harvard Business School Press, 2000) explains how both big company personnel and entrepreneurs learn how to reconfigure market spaces, find new sources of differentiation, and seize the enormous potential of market breakthroughs. The number one thing to take from the book is that you must eliminate paralyzing uncertainty by thinking and acting like an entrepreneur. In all, this is a great book for both big company personnel and potential OPM entrepreneurs.

Once you have a large group of examples of deals somewhat similar to an OPM deal, you are prepared to discuss the concept of your contact branching out and proceeding to launch an OPM arrangement in which he or she is the OPM entrepreneur.

At this point your contact will probably ask why your company doesn't just pay the contact to set everything up. Even though there certainly might be a big reward if the venture works out, why should he or she take the risk? In other words, if you believe in the idea so much, why doesn't your company follow through with an investment? The answer really is in two parts: first, the company doesn't have the ability to move ahead; and second, the concept of hiring a middleman is too new for the company to accept as a viable up-front investment. The reason a company isn't able to move ahead on its own could be that it doesn't understand the customers well enough, doesn't have personnel to pursue the idea, doesn't have enough money, or doesn't have the right marketing or manufacturing capabilities. And why not just hire the middleman? One reason is that the whole concept of hiring a middleman is too new to most companies, and it will take the company too long to act, especially if it has to agree to pay the middleman. Other reasons companies won't hire a middleman are that the company wants to see that the middleman believes enough in the idea to invest in it, and that, because the company isn't sure how the deal will eventually work out with an unknown middleman, it isn't willing to risk an investment.

Once you feel that you have credible answers to any objections that might be raised, pick three or four examples from your market that are somewhat close to your situation. You are then ready to meet with the person you hope to convince to take the OPM entrepreneur role. You can start by explaining the situations you've chosen in the market, and then tell your contact that you feel there is an opportunity for the contact to take the lead role in putting the deal together. You need to make the following points.

1. An opportunity exists.

2. The opportunity is not that different from what other people have already done in the market.

3. You are willing to strongly consider being the marketing (or manufacturing) partner if the individual can pull the deal together.

4. You will help in any way you can.

5. You need someone outside the company to take the lead role, or the project just won't happen.

PROJECTS TO OFFER

OPM entrepreneurs can do virtually any type of project, but you obviously don't want to offer a project that could have major impact on the market and that could greatly enhance your market position. You want to do that type of project on your own. A project like that has too many benefits to share, unless you don't have enough resources to do it yourself. Even then you probably should strike out on your own to form a partnership or alliance without a middleman.

Major market-changing projects come around only rarely. More often the projects you will come across are smaller, and the ones you don't proceed with on your own will be potential OPM entrepreneur projects. You still need to be selective, however. Your company can only handle a certain number of projects, and so you want to be selective in choosing projects to propose to a contact as an OPM project.

In my experience, you should proceed when projects have one or more of these three characteristics for marketing companies.

1. *The project strengthens your entire product line in the eyes of the distribution network.* That means the project will produce sales dividends across your entire line. A project will strengthen the product line if it helps your line be a better customer solution, or if customers perceive that your product is best in a key product or service category.

2. *The project strengthens your ties to customers.* For example, this could be the result if the project provides an exclusive maintenance service in an important area. Other examples are a project that is developed as a response to input from important market influencers, or is a product that could be endorsed by someone important to your customers.

3. *The project could increase sales 25 percent or more.*

A provider should proceed to find potential OPM contacts when projects have one or more of the following characteristics:

1. *The project can offer you secure production for a minimum of three to five years.* If the project is short term, it isn't much better than a contract manufacturing deal, which won't provide you with a future any more secure than what you have today.

2. *The project can easily be made with your existing equipment and requires a minimum investment.*

3. *The project can increase your in-plant production at least 25 percent while requiring only minimum additional investment.*

I've consulted and talked with dozens of companies and OPM-type entrepreneurs. Companies are typically challenged by rapid change and are fearful of what lies ahead, while OPM-style entrepreneurs embrace rapid change because that change creates market opportunities. The companies that are true winners over the next ten years will be the ones that will also learn to embrace change. Even when their resources are small, companies can capitalize on market changes by taking advantage of the rapidly growing numbers of OPM entrepreneurs. Start your own network of contacts, offer them attractive opportunities, and just watch what happens. I expect that you will soon find your market share and profits moving up as, every year, you launch one or two deals with OPM entrepreneurs.

Appendix A

GLOSSARY

ADVISORY COUNCILS

A group of people, which could include company and industry personnel, that offers advice to a company or group on a regular basis.

ALLIANCES

An agreement between two companies to assist each other's businesses. KLM and Northwest Airlines have an alliance that helps the companies feed each other's U.S. and European feeder networks.

AMORTIZE

To turn a large payment into a series of smaller payments related to shipments. A $10,000 tooling cost is amortized if it is recouped by adding an extra fifty cents per unit to the unit production costs for each unit produced.

ANNUAL RETURN

The annual profit percentage generated by an investment. A $10,000 profit on a $100,000 investment is a 10 percent annual return.

BETA TESTING

Product testing with real customers to ensure that a product works as designed.

BRANDED PRODUCTS

Products sold under a proprietary name, which could be product or service related, such as the George Foreman Grill, or a company-related name such as Trek bikes.

BREAKEVEN CAPACITY

The capacity, given as a percentage of total capacity, at which a company covers all of its manufacturing and fixed costs. For example, "seventy breakeven capacity" indicates that the company must be running at 70 percent of its rated capacity in order to break even.

BROKER

Someone who arranges the purchase or sale of products and services without taking ownership of the goods or services.

BUY-AND-SELL AGREEMENTS

An agreement for one party to buy and another party to sell a product or service.

BUYOUT PROVISIONS

A clause in an agreement contract that stipulates how a party's interest in the agreement can be bought out by the other party or parties.

COMPARATIVE RESEARCH

Research in which people compare products for similar uses or compare the value of products used in similar applications.

CONFIDENTIALITY AGREEMENTS

Agreements in which signing parties agree not to disclose confidential information obtained by the other party in the agreement. Also referred to as *non-disclosure agreements*.

CONTRACT MANUFACTURER

A manufacturer that agrees to make another manufacturer's, marketer's, or entrepreneur's product for a fee.

CO-OP ADVERTISING

Promotional program in which a supplier agrees to pay for part of the costs of a retailer's, distributor's, or dealer's advertising programs when the supplier's products or services are included in the advertising.

CREDIT LINE

The amount of money that a company can borrow from a bank without applying for an additional loan. It is a loan reserve set aside by the bank for the customer, who doesn't need to pay interest until the money is borrowed.

DERIVATIVE PRODUCTS

Also referred to as *next-generation products*, they are products based on improvements to an original product for either performance or durability.

DISBURSEMENT

Money that is distributed by one party in a two- or three-party agreement to the other party or parties, often paid upon customer payment or on a monthly, quarterly, or yearly basis.

DISTRIBUTION CHANNEL

A series of companies that take a product or service from the producer to the end user. A music CD distribution channel might include distributors, manufacturers' sales agents, and retailers.

DOCUMENT DISCLOSURE PROGRAM

A program of the U.S. Patent Office that allows you to register an idea to establish an effective date of invention. For more details see the Web site *www.uspto.gov/web/offices/pac/disdo.html.*

FOCUS GROUPS

A group of end users, distributors, or retailers brought together to evaluate a product or service.

GROSS MARGIN

The percentage of a product's sales price that is profit. A 40 percent margin indicates that 40 percent of the product's price is profit. On a $100 sale, a 40 percent margin indicates that $40 is profit and $60 covers the production costs of the product or service.

INDEMNIFICATION

A clause that protects you from having to paying damages to another party.

INFILTRATION MARKETING

Tactics that put marketers and companies into the customers' world. Hosting events, running classes and seminars, and sponsoring customer activities are all part of infiltration marketing.

INTELLECTUAL PROPERTY

The only defined intellectual properties in the United States are copyrights, patents, and trademarks. Other people can't use intellectual property without the owner's permission.

JOINT VENTURE

A separate legal entity set up by several companies to market a product or service. Typically a joint venture has its own management and is started with funding provided by all of the joint-venture stakeholders.

LEAD TIME

The time between when an order is placed and when it will be shipped or delivered.

LETTER OF INTENT

A letter that expresses a party's intent to move ahead with an agreement. This is typically used during the investigative stage of a new concept to show that the parties signing the letter have a strong intent to move ahead if positive results come out of their investigations.

LICENSE AGREEMENT

An agreement whereby the owner of intellectual property allows another person or company to use its intellectual property in return for a payment arrangement, which is usually a royalty.

MARKET INFLUENCERS

People considered by others in the market to be experts or large sellers or buyers. Speakers, researchers, or the initial developers of a concept or idea in the market often are considered market influencers.

MARKET SPACE

Refers to a market, typically defined by a customer group, application, or a distribution channel, that a company competes in or for.

MARKUP

The percentage a company raises its prices over its costs. A 50 percent markup indicates that the costs are raised by 50 percent to determine the company's price to its customers. If costs are $100, adding a 50 percent markup would set the price at $150.

MEMORANDUM OF UNDERSTANDING

An agreement similar to a letter of intent in that it is used to show that companies have serious interest in working together to explore a business opportunity prior to a final agreement being signed.

NICHE MARKET

A segment of a market that is usually categorized by a specific application or a customer group with special needs or concerns.

NON-DISCLOSURE AGREEMENTS

An agreement wherein one or both parties agree not to disclose to third parties any confidential information that has been obtained in the normal course of business.

OBSERVATIONAL RESEARCH

Research obtained by watching end users perform tasks related to a product or service.

OVERHEAD

Any expense that is not related to producing a product or service; administrative salaries, rent, insurance, utilities, and professional fees are examples. Also referred to as *fixed costs*.

OVERHEAD ABSORPTION

Describes the process by which a company pays for its overhead costs by allocating part of the cost to individual units of products and/or services.

PERIPHERAL PRODUCTS

Products that are accessories for a main product, or that are used in conjunction with the main product to accomplish a goal. An edge trimmer is a peripheral product to a lawn mower, because both are used to maintain a well-kept lawn.

PREORDERS

Orders obtained for a product or service before a company is in production. Preorders often have six months' to one-year lead time.

PRESS RELEASE

Information sent out to the news media, which could include magazines and newspapers as well as radio and TV stations.

PRICE/VALUE RELATIONSHIP

A comparison of the price actually charged compared to a product's value as perceived by end users or customers. A good price/value relationship exists when the price is lower than a product or service's perceived value.

PRIVATE LABEL

A product is private labeled when it is designed and created by one company and then sold by another company under that company's name. The Sears Kenmore line is a private-label line. Another manufacturer creates and produces the product, which Sears agrees to sell under its name.

PRODUCT LIABILITY INSURANCE

Insurance that pays for damages that might occur to either property or persons from a product or service. OPM entrepreneurs may need this insurance even though their manufacturing or marketing partners have their own product liability insurance.

PRODUCT LINE

Refers to all of the products that a company carries for a particular application. A company with an outdoor painting product line might have paints, brushes, rollers, sprays, and window guards in its product line.

PROFIT MARGINS

The percentage of a company's sales dollars that is profit after all expenses are deducted. Also referred to as *net margin*.

PROTOTYPES

A representation of the final product both in appearance and in function.

RIGHT OF FIRST REFUSAL

When one party in an agreement offers this right, it is agreeing to give the other party the first right to participate in a new product or service, as defined in the agreement, before the product or service is offered to anyone else.

ROYALTY

A payment made to the owner of intellectual property for the right to use that property.

SALES CHANNEL

Similar to a distribution channel, it refers to a listing of all of the companies or individuals who play a role in the product's moving from a producer to a final customer.

SALES OUTLETS

Refers to the number of places or ways in which a product or service could be bought.

SAMPLING

The practice of giving out free samples of food or products at a retail location or event attended by potential customers.

SOURCING AGENTS

Companies or individuals who locate overseas suppliers for U.S. companies. Typically, these agents specialize in acquiring products or services from one or two countries.

START-UP COSTS

The total cost of introducing a product or service, including initial production runs, tooling, product development costs, and operating capital.

TOOLING

Parts or accessories that are added to a piece of production equipment to make a specific part. A plastic mold that is used with injection molding equipment to make a specific part is tooling. A metal pattern used with a stamping machine to make a specified part is also considered tooling.

TRADE MAGAZINE

A magazine geared to companies and individuals in the industry, who may be retailers, distributors, or producers. The magazine is geared to an audience that produces or markets products or services to end users.

TRADE SHOWS

Conventions or conferences geared to industry personnel rather than to end users or consumers.

Appendix B

Sample Agreements: Non-Disclosure Agreement, Mutual Confidentiality Agreement, and Letter of Intent (LOI)

These agreements are provided to help your understanding of what the documents will be like for your own deals. The Non-Disclosure Agreement and Mutual Confidentiality Agreement are fairly straightforward. Final LOIs, on the other hand, can be confusing. I've written the sample LOI in this appendix in straightforward, easy-to-understand language that is not full of the legalese you see so often in contracts. That is to help you understand what an LOI is accomplishing and to help you negotiate the terms of an LOI with your partner.

Note: While these agreements are typical of the ones you may use, you may still want to consult with your attorney prior to submitting any documents to ensure that they have the correct legal language for your state. You will also probably need to modify sections of the agreements to fit your circumstances.

SIMPLE NON-DISCLOSURE AGREEMENT

You don't want to scare away your market research and initial industry contacts with a long Non-Disclosure Agreement. A short, simpler agreement is just as effective.

Non-Disclosure Agreement

This is a Non-Disclosure Agreement (Agreement), effective <u>(date of agreement)</u> between <u>(your name)</u> of <u>(your address)</u> (the Discloser) and <u>(the contact's name)</u> of <u>(Recipient's address)</u> (the Recipient).

Background

The Discloser desires to have the Recipient review and evaluate <u>(your concept description)</u> to help determine the concept's market viability. The Discloser agrees to disclose to the Recipient certain information necessary for the Recipient to understand the concept; how it will work for the end user; how it will be sold through distribution; and how it will compare to competitive features and pricing.

Terms

"Confidential Information" is information that the Discloser regards as confidential. It includes <u>(list here what you will disclose; for example, the concept itself—both its description and use—as well as business information, ad layouts, pricing data, and market research interviews)</u>. Confidential Information includes only information disclosed to the Recipient for one year from the date of this Agreement.

Confidential Information does not include:

a. Information available in the public domain from written publications, trade-show attendance, offers to sell through sales literature, or any other effort that is not the result of activities of the Recipient.

b. Information that was known by the Recipient prior to the disclosure of this document. *(Note: clauses b and c are not typically necessary for consumer non-disclosures, but you should include them when talking to people in the industry.)*

c. Information that is disclosed to the Recipient by a third party without a confidentiality agreement and without a violation of this Agreement by the Recipient.

The Recipient agrees to hold in confidence all Confidential Information and to not disclose it to other parties without the written permission of the Discloser.

We the undersigned do hereby agree to abide by the conditions of this Agreement.

Recipient Signature   Discloser Signature

Date   Date

MUTUAL CONFIDENTIALITY AGREEMENT

This statement is one you would use with a partner in combination with a Letter of Intent (LOI). This form is for situations in which you are disclosing information to a potential partner with the intent to form a final agreement. This form is completed so that it is easier to understand.

Mutual Confidentiality Agreement

This Mutual Confidentiality Agreement is made and entered into (the Agreement), May 28, 2005, by Don Debelak of P.O. Box 120861, New Brighton, MN 55112 (Debelak) and Reardon Advertising, a Minnesota corporation (Reardon).

Background

A. Debelak writes magazine columns and books and is a marketing consultant for a wide range of companies that market to consumers and industrial accounts, many of whom actively advertise in both trade and consumer magazines. Debelak has procured the rights to the Pouch-Up, a light cardboard insert that holds CDs and DVDs for magazines and pops up into a pyramid when the page is open, presenting the CD or DVD to the reader.

B. Reardon sells inserts, which it designs and prints, for easy inclusion into a magazine upon printing. Reardon's clients are magazine advertising departments that sell high-impact advertising inserts to their clients. Reardon is interested in actively promoting the Pouch-Up to its clients as a new, high-impact magazine insert.

Whereas, Debelak is the owner of certain intellectual and confidential property (Confidential Property) concerning the Pouch-Up and related technical know-how and desires to explore the possibility of entering into a contractual agreement with Reardon, and

Whereas, Reardon desires to receive said Confidential Property for the purpose of evaluating the idea and to consider entering into a contractual arrangement with Debelak concerning the Confidential Property, and

Whereas, Debelak is willing to provide Reardon with said Confidential Property for the stated evaluation purposes under the terms stated herein,

Thereby the parties agree to be legally bound as follows.

1. This Agreement shall apply to all Confidential Information disclosed by or on behalf of either party to the other parties, including without limitation, each party's employees, agents, consultants, officers, directors, attorneys, and accountants. Both parties further agree that it will not use or disclose to any third party, nor permit the use by or disclosure to any third party, of any Confidential Information obtained from or disclosed by the other party unless it receives approval of the other party and has a signed statement of the third party on file.

2. "Confidential Information" means all information disclosed by or on behalf of either party to the other concerning either party's business or any product or service developed (or proposed to be developed) by the disclosing party, whether such information is disclosed in writing, verbally, or by inspection. Confidential Information may include, but is not limited to, product designs, patent applications, requisitions, instructions, product and manufacturing technology, supplier data, marketing plans and consumer data, customer lists, cost and expense data, trade secrets, processes, methods, know-how, techniques, and similar information, and any and all

notes, reports, studies, memorandums, or other documents derived or developed in any way.

Confidential Information shall not include:

a. Information that at the time of disclosure is in the public domain or is otherwise available to the receiving party other than on a confidential basis;

b. Information that, after disclosure, becomes a part of the public domain by publication or otherwise through no fault of the receiving party;

c. Information disclosed to the receiving party by a third party not under an obligation of confidentiality to the disclosing party; or

d. Information that is or has been developed by the receiving party independent of the disclosures by the disclosing party.

3. In the event the parties' discussions terminate, or upon the earlier request of the either disclosing party, the receiving party shall immediately return to the disclosing party all documents, other written information, and tangible objects obtained from the disclosing party containing Confidential Information and any materials created or derived from Confidential Information without retaining any copies.

4. In the event the discussions between Debelak and Reardon do not result in a Transaction or any other business arrangement, or if such a Transaction or arrangement is negotiated but not initiated, the confidentiality obligation shall survive the termination of such discussions and negotiations.

5. Ownership and Assignment of Inventions. No right or license, either express or implied, under any patent, trademark,

copyright, trade secret, or intellectual property right of any kind is granted with this Agreement.

6. Nothing in this Agreement shall constitute a commitment or obligation by either party to consummate a future agreement to proceed. All Reardon developments, designs, improvements, inventions, techniques, know-how, data, or other information of possible technical or commercial importance relating to the Pouch-Up made, conceived, reduced to practice, or learned as a result of Reardon's access to Debelak's confidential information shall be the sole property of Debelak.

7. This Agreement shall not be amended or supplemented other than by a written instrument referring specifically to this Agreement and signed by all parties.

8. No right or license, either express or implied, under any patent, trademark, copyright, trade secret, or intellectual property right of any kind is granted in this Agreement.

9. The laws of the State of Minnesota shall govern the validity, construction, enforcement, and interpretation of this Agreement.

10. Entire Agreement. This Agreement constitutes the entire agreement between the parties and supersedes and cancels any and all prior agreements, written or oral, between them relating to the Pouch-Up.

11. Relationship of Parties. Nothing in this Agreement, its provisions, or a future agreement constitutes that either party to this Agreement is an agent, employee, or legal representative for the other party, nor shall any party to this Agreement suggest it is other than an independent agent to other parties. This Agreement does not create and shall not be deemed to create a relationship

of partners, associates, or principal and agent between the parties hereto, and the parties acknowledge that they each are acting as principals.

12. If any provision of this Agreement is held to be illegal, invalid, or unenforceable under present or future law effective during the term hereof, such provision shall be fully severable and this Agreement shall be construed and enforced as if such illegal, invalid, or unenforceable provision never comprised a part of the Agreement, and the remaining provisions shall remain in full force and effect.

In Witness whereof, the parties execute this Agreement on May 28, 2005.

Debelak

By:_____

Don Debelak

Reardon Advertising

By:_____

Jeff McKinney

Title: Vice President of Marketing

LETTER OF INTENT (LOI)

This is a sample Letter of Intent agreement that you would use along with a Mutual Confidentiality Agreement. I've used the same two parties as in the Mutual Confidentiality Agreement so you can see how the two documents tie together.

Letter of Intent

This Letter of Intent is made and entered into (the Agreement) May 28, 2005, by Don Debelak of P.O. Box 120861, New Brighton, MN 55112 (Debelak) and Reardon Advertising, a Minnesota corporation (Reardon).

A. Debelak is a marketing consultant for a wide range of companies that market to consumers and industrial accounts, many of whom actively advertise in both trade and consumer magazines. Debelak has procured the rights to the Pouch-Up, a light cardboard insert that holds CDs and DVDs for magazines and pops up into a pyramid when the page is open, presenting the CD or DVD to the reader. Debelak has conducted market interviews and research that indicate the product has wide appeal to customers and has sought out and found several manufacturers capable of producing a high-quality version of the product on a cost-effective basis.

B. Reardon sells inserts, as well as designing and printing the inserts, for easy inclusion into a magazine upon printing. Reardon's clients are magazine advertising departments that sell high-impact advertising inserts to their advertising clients. Reardon is interested in actively promoting the Pouch-Up to its clients as a new, high-impact magazine insert. Reardon has fourteen sales representatives and a four-person marketing staff and effectively markets to a twenty-two state region, primarily east of the Mississippi River, and has sales of over $42 million per year.

Whereas the parties agree to investigate the development of a business relationship to exploit the market potential of the Pouch-Up and leverage the combined expertise, capabilities, contacts, and market knowledge, and

Whereas the parties agree that Debelak is expected to assist in market development and promotion; coordinate product introduction tasks; and facilitate the marketing and manufacturing partner interactions,

Therefore, in recognition of their mutual interests and desires, the Parties do here declare by this LOI their intent to negotiate in good faith, mutually agreeable terms and conditions to be included in a formal binding agreement between the two parties to be concluded at a later date. The Parties set forth the following non-binding principles which are to be negotiated in the formal agreement.

The terms and conditions for the Parties to this LOI are:

1. Overview of Future Agreement
    a. Reardon and Debelak will work together to market Pouch-Up to marketers and advertisers that use consumer and trade print publications. Reardon and Debelak will use a significant portion of their resources to promote the Pouch-Up, Reardon assigning sales and marketing people with the proper resources and Debelak providing sales training, assistance on major calls, and minor product variations to meet customers' needs.
    b. Three-year minimum agreement with cancellation clauses for nonperformance.
    c. Debelak will ensure manufacturing capabilities are available, with Reardon having the right to approve the final manufacturer based on its quality and ability to meet demand.

d. All major decisions regarding the changes to the product including performance, benefits, appearance, and features must be approved by Reardon and Debelak.

e. Reardon will approve final standard product specifications and will provide final product specifications for each order.

f. Reardon will purchase product on standard 30-day payment terms from Debelak, who will acquire it from one or more manufacturing suppliers.

g. Reardon will have exclusive rights to market the Pouch-Up provided it meets the minimum volume requirements of the agreement.

h. Reardon and Debelak agree to offer the other party the right of first refusal for opportunities that develop as a result of the marketing of the Pouch-Up.

2. Roles and Responsibilities

a. Reardon responsibilities include sales and marketing to potential clients, offering quarterly and yearly forecasts, detailed input regarding the specifications for each order, and providing input regarding product specifications and performance.

b. Debelak's responsibilities include providing the Pouch-Up product concept, know-how, production methods, and business and market information; providing sales training and assistance; working with Reardon to provide modified Pouch-Ups to meet specific customers' requirements; securing manufacturing; coordinating as required the product launch; and subsequent coordination between Reardon and the manufacturing organizations producing the Pouch-Up.

3. Proprietary Information
    a. All information exchanged by the parties is subject to the Mutual Confidentiality Agreement which is already in place and which is attached as Exhibit A.
    b. All intellectual property regarding the Pouch-Up is owned by Debelak, and a patent regarding the Pouch-Up has been filed with the United States Patent and Trademark Office.
    c. Debelak makes no warranties as to the validity of the patent rights, but does warrant that the patent application identified above is on file in the United States Patent and Trademark Office.
    d. Debelak warrants he has sole rights to enter into agreements regarding the Pouch-Up.

4. Any notice given regarding this agreement shall be in writing and shall be effective on the date mailed by certified mail, receipt requested:

If to Debelak

  Don Debelak
  P.O. Box 120861
  New Brighton, MN 55112

If to Reardon

  Jeff McKinney
  Reardon Advertising
  8645 Country Road, NE
  Little Canada, MN 55116

5. Expenses. Each party will bear all of its own travel expenses. Reardon will fund any major market research or promotional campaigns run to support the Pouch-Up. Neither party will make any claims or charges against the other unless mutually agreed to in advance by both parties.

6. Nature of the Agreement. This LOI shall not be construed to create a joint venture or any other form of business organization of any kind between the parties. At all times the parties shall remain independent contractors, each responsible for its own employees.

7. The laws of the State of Minnesota shall govern the validity, construction, enforcement, and interpretation of this Agreement.

8. Entire Agreement. This Agreement constitutes the entire agreement between the parties and supersedes and cancels any and all prior agreements, with the exception of the Mutual Confidentiality Agreement, written or oral, between them relating to the Pouch-Up.

9. The effective date of this LOI is May 28, 2005. If a definitive agreement is not executed on mutually agreeable terms by November 1, 2005, then the proposed relationship in the LOI shall terminate; however, parties will still be governed by the responsibilities, obligations, and covenants set forth in the Mutual Confidentiality Agreement (which will continue in full force and effect).

In Witness whereof, the parties hereto have cause this LOI to be executed in duplicate the day and year written below.

Don Debelak   Reardon Advertising

By:_____   By:_____
Don Debelak   Jeff McKinney
                                Vice President of Marketing

_____   _____
Date   Date

Index

ABOUT THE AUTHOR

Don Debelak is a new product-marketing specialist who has more than two decades of experience as a consultant for small businesses and start-up ventures. Mr. Debelak has established himself as a leader at spotting emerging business trends. He is the author of several popular books, including *How to Bring Your Product to Market for Less Than $5,000*. Mr. Debelak has been featured in the *Wall Street Journal* and the *Washington Post*. He lives in Minneapolis, MN.